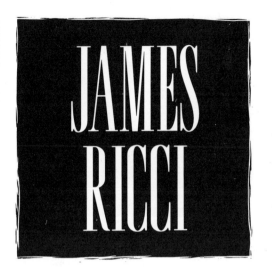

JAMES RICCI

LOOK AT IT THIS WAY

Detroit Free Press

Editor: *Marty Claus*

Cover and chapter page design: *Andrew J. Hartley*

Copy editing and research: *Susan Hall-Balduf*

Proofreading: *Geralynn Lama, Barb Arrigo*

Cover photograph: *Tony Spina*

Chapter illustrations: *Stephanie Shieldhouse*

Printed in U.S.A. on recycled paper

ISBN 0-937247-24-3

Contents

CHAPTER 3: LOOK AT IT THIS WAY

CHAPTER 4: MEN AND WOMEN

CHAPTER 5: SONG OF MY OWN SELF

CHAPTER 6: OTHER LIVES

CHAPTER 7: AT HOME

POSTCARD

Introduction

Readers often ask me (usually right after patting me on the back or wagging a finger in my face) where I get my column ideas.

The answer is: directly from God.

I wish.

Really, column ideas are like lost car keys and former lovers. You can never tell where they'll turn up. I find my ideas in everything from the biggest news story of the day to the smirk on the face of one of my teenage daughters when she entertains the notion of middle-aged people having sex. I find them in newspaper and magazine articles, letters and telephone calls from readers, and the off-hand remarks of colleagues and friends. I find them in the more profound experiences of my own pretty ordinary life, and in the ruthless silliness that sometimes commandeers my brain, usually when I'm pondering topics of grave public importance.

Whatever the source of the ideas, I try to make sure the columns that result are both compelling and unique, or, at least, uniquely mine. I think the columns in this book meet that test, which is why I selected them from the 500 or so I've written for the Detroit Free Press since December 1988. I hope you agree.

This book doesn't have a dedication because I couldn't think of where to start in selecting people for the honor. I could hardly list the names of all the members of my family whose privacy I've betrayed in print, or of all my helpful friends and colleagues, or of all the perfect strangers who've submitted to being written about by me. I'd be an ingrate, however, not to mention how indebted I am to Marty Claus, who edited this book, A.J. Hartley, who designed it, and Tony Spina, who made the cover photograph.

It's gratifying to see my work between the covers of a book. Funny how typography can enhance a piece of writing. Hmm. That gives me an idea ...

NEXT
OF KIN

CHAPTER ONE

Marital Gold

En route to church to say their vows, the couple sat in the back seat of the car trying to expel their tenseness in long, ragged sighs.

"Oh, no, I forgot my rings," she said. "And my rosary."

"I'm more nervous now than I was the first time," he said miserably.

"I hate being the center of attention," she said after a while.

The replacement best man tried to be worthy of his designation. "Mom, Dad," I said from behind the wheel. "Try not to let yourselves get all wrought up. Think of this as an excuse for a party."

We pulled up to the plain, red brick church of St. Anthony where, 50 years and two days before, my mother and father formally launched a venture in love, optimism, confusion, hurt and delight that numbered among its subsidiaries my ever-loving life.

The old wedding photos show my parents as small, trim people with shining skin and an overall handsomeness none of their three children equaled. He was a steelworker, she a dime-store clerk. His new Hart, Schaffner and Marx suit cost $19. They took the bus to Cleveland for their honeymoon. The hotel bill was $4.

The 50th anniversary celebration brought relatives from all over the country to our gray hometown on the Ohio River to marvel at the longevity of their relationship.

Marriage has become one of modern life's most difficult feats to sustain. How had my parents' endured so long?

There's been plenty of love in their marriage, to be sure, but there is plenty of that in marriages that unravel far sooner. I think you must look not at what's been present in it so much as what's been absent.

A key absence was that of self-consciousness. That's why they were nervous last weekend — everybody so pointedly thinking about their life together and their having to participate in the public marking of it.

Their marriage has been devoid also of unrealistic demands. They didn't expect their spouse to be best friend, closest confidant, wisest counselor, most creative lover, cleverest conversationalist, optimal income producer and most challenging tennis opponent. They had kids early, and their attention never became pitilessly focused on the imperfect being occupying the other side of the bed.

My father never indulged in self-dramatizing harangues about how my mother failed to meet this or that emotional need of his at this or that critical moment. He just went bowling.

My mother didn't berate my father for not giving her enough space to grow to her true potential. She just gave us baths.

They knew exactly who they were, did their best and forgave each other their worst. They laughed when there was something to laugh about, cried when there was something to cry about. Overall, laughed far more often than cried.

They both worked very hard, and never doubted the correctness of their mission, which was to do right by the kids.

And every other Saturday or so they'd go out together, he shrugging smoothly in his suit, fixing the brim of his hat slightly down over one eye, she dolled to the nines, rouged and chewing a half-stick of Doublemint to sweeten her breath. Handsome, cake-top figures again.

Another Decade Summed Up

Yo, Uncle.

Didn't we just do this? I mean, 1950, 1960, 1970, 1980, 1990. How many times do I have to tell you?

YES, I EXIST!

I'd think you'd be able to keep track of that little fact from my tax returns. A few years ago, when I mistakenly declared "other income" on the same line as "wages, salaries, tips, etc." on my IRS 1040, you certainly perked up to my existence. If I ever neglected to file altogether I'd bet you'd prove to know exactly who I was and where to find me.

Even if I'd died since 1980, you'd have been among the first to find out. I can just see the IRS swooping down consolingly on my widow and orphans to make certain the life insurance benefits were properly diminished for the greater good of the Drug Enforcement Administration, the Library of Congress, and the U.S. Geological Survey, not to mention the Quayle vice presidency.

I'm probably taking this a little too personally, but after serving in the military, voting in federal elections and exposing myself to inclusion on federal court juries, it's a little irritating to have to fill out a Census Bureau form to officially demonstrate my being.

On the other hand, I suppose you have a right to an updated form on my household. Things have indeed changed a bit since 1980.

So let's get to it:

Person 1. Yes. That would be me. Good old Male/white/43/now married/no (not Spanish/Hispanic). You'd know me anywhere. Come to think of it, maybe you wouldn't. Hair a bit thinner, waist a little thicker, energy and optimism about a half-quart low and in occasional need of performance-enhancing additive. Increasingly a trial to ...

Person 2. Wife/female/white/44/now married/no (not Spanish/ Hispanic), who must seek to balance expanding churlishness of Person 1 with growing demands on patience and future financial stability presented by ...

Person 3. Natural-born or adopted daughter/white/16/never married/no (not Spanish/Hispanic). This person seems to be absorbing a far greater share of household energies since the last census.

Of course, you would have known her in those days as Natural born or adopted daughter/white/6/etc./etc. Her principal concern then was not which college hit-and-miss principal breadwinner Person 1 could afford to send her to, but learning to ride a two-wheel bike (which problem Person 1 handled with a lot more aplomb than he is the present one).

But enough of Person 3. She is clearly on her way out of the household anyway, pursued by the rapidly drumming footsteps of ...

Person 4. Natural born or adopted daughter/white/13/never married/no (not Spanish/Hispanic). This is the one now identifiable by the telephone receiver permanently fused to one ear, thereby leaving hands free for air-guitaring to the loud music that seems to swirl about her wherever she goes, like some auditory perfume put on way too strong.

There's more to tell — hopes, fears, victories, defeats — but you really didn't leave enough space to write in, what with all these line items and tiny circles. Besides, I've got to get started on that other form, the one you're expecting by April 15. If it's a little late this year, there won't be any problem, right?

A Newborn Older Sister

In a sense, I witnessed the birth of my older sister.

It took place on a chill, bright day last month in Michigan Stadium, with several thousand spectators applauding in the stands.

The period of gestation for this birth was halting and difficult and lasted 27 years; I was a witness to it, too.

Virginia, whom we have always called Ginger, is five years older than I. As a girl, she loved playing the older sister, the teacher. She was in fourth grade when she taught me, who had not been sent to kindergarten, how to read. (I won the reading medal in first grade the next year.) She walked me to the small public library in our town and helped me get my first borrowing card. She showed me how to keep my concentration (eyes shut, fingers plugging ears) while singing harmony with someone else.

After I'd entered high school, she was determined to prevent my being consigned to that blighted category of adolescence, the unpopular. There wasn't much for her to work with — a mournful, self-conscious freshman of 13 who didn't know how to dance. Ginger, however, was undaunted. On the eve of my first high school dance — she was the one who had insisted I go — she lugged her old blue-and-white plastic record player to the basement and then lugged (and prodded and pushed) me across the green-speckled tile floor until I could manage a passable imitation of the jitterbug and slow dance.

She had been an A-student through grade school, but in high school she enrolled in a commercial, rather than college preparatory, course of study. Between her and my parents, it was somehow understood that she was bound for the working world immediately after high school. It was 1959, and she was caught on a cusp between generations. It was still rare for girls from blue-collar, ethnic families in small steel-mill towns to go to college; just a few years later, it was not.

So she took her A-average and her high school shorthand medal into the steel mill where my father worked. She was placed in an old brick office building made the color of dried blood by flue dust from the nearby open-hearth furnaces. She did secretarial work, and waited; waited for the right man to come along, for the babies, for the proscribed life that was destined to be hers.

I was the one who went to college.

I was the one who went to graduate school, learned a foreign language, traveled abroad, entered a profession.

Over the years, my relationship with my sister underwent a subtle reversal.

I became the one listened to, the one with experiences to relate and things to teach. Proud of how far I'd come, wanting to dazzle her, I wrote long letters from abroad. When we were together, I wrapped her in long monologues about studies, about work, about my prospects (never, of course, about my doubts and failures). More than anyone in my family, she was deeply interested, living each step vicariously.

Eventually, she married a paper products salesman and moved to a town 30 miles from our hometown. Secretarial work increasingly bored her. After her first daughter came, Ginger conformed to the life of full-time mother as all the women in her line had done.

But she felt something amiss. She had a sense of unaddressed possibilities stirring within her. At her husband's suggestion, she enrolled in a course at the local branch campus of a state university. It had been a decade since she'd graduated from high school.

Five years later, fitting studies into the interstices of a family life that now included a second daughter, she completed the equivalent of two years in college. By then, her older daughter was in school all day, which enabled Ginger to enroll full time at the university's main branch. Every day for two years, she commuted 60 miles with her younger daughter, who attended nursery school at the university.

In 1976, 17 years after she'd finished high school, she was awarded a bachelor of arts degree in English. Her final grade-point average was 3.85.

The next year, she got a job teaching English to high school seniors in a small Ohio high school. She threw herself into the work and couldn't fathom teachers who didn't see its excitement and importance.

She was on a roll. She began postgraduate studies at a nearby university and finished her master of arts in English in two years. At the urging of faculty members impressed by her hard work and enthusiasm, she countenanced the unthinkable, but eminently logical, conclusion — a PhD.

She was one of four persons selected in 1982 for a joint English and education doctoral program at the University of Michigan.

Going was not an easy decision. She would have to live apart from her daughters, now teenagers and in special need of her presence; her husband would be doubly burdened, earning the family's living by himself and keeping the household running. Some in my family did not want her to go; they feared the strain on the marriage.

The old expectations, the traditional ways, sent dark birds of guilt circling low over her.

But she went.

She was 41 years old and had never lived on her own. The apartment she took in Ann Arbor was small and sparsely furnished. Within its walls, she went *mano a mano* with the unaccustomed loneliness and the uneasiness of being surrounded by much younger peers, many with degrees from Ivy League universities. With the crushing workload of a doctoral candidate, there was barely enough time for a few hours of sleep at night.

But she always had time for me.

Whenever I visited she seemed wrung out, running on the fumes of her passion for her goal. Her words came in prolonged gushes. All the time in the world was not enough for her even to begin to say all that had to be said, about her professors, her freshman composition students, about Faulkner and Henry James, about how young people's natural affinity for literature was subverted by teachers.

The precision of her thought and the analytical quality of her mind bloomed and billowed all around us. I had trouble keeping up.

She was the same person, but an expanded version. Her learning and what it took to acquire it had swelled her understanding and insight. I found myself talking to her — not of my work, but of the fears and misgivings and uncertainties I had amassed in two decades of adult life. She listened and understood, and helped where she could. Where she couldn't, she ached a little along with me. We became intimates, confidants; our telephone calls seldom lasted less than an hour.

She got through her time in Ann Arbor with all her banners flying. She had two articles published in professional journals. She was nominated by the English department for the outstanding teaching assistant award (no surprise to me). She finished in two years an amount of classroom work that normally takes four.

On returning home, she gave herself one year to complete her dissertation. Its title was "Young Adult Literature and Reader Response: A Descriptive Study of Students and Teachers," and it was finished in 12 months. She dedicated it to my mother and father.

Commencement was held May 3 at Michigan Stadium. Among the thousands of gowned graduates, only the new PhDs were summoned individually, in alphabetical order, to the dais. Dr. Virginia Ricci Monseau, late of the steel-mill secretarial pool, was the 113th called.

Her hand was shaken by the president of the university, her degree was conferred; thus fully credentialed, she was dispatched to a new incarnation as assistant professor of English at Youngstown State University.

I stood and applauded hard. For the lesson she'd given me in indomitability. For a memory of first-grade reading medals and makeshift basement dance floors. For my good fortune of having a big sister again.

The Girls Come First

I remember distinctly when my daughters were in the womb, although I didn't know they were daughters at the time.

I tracked them as closely as I could, read up on the transformations that were occurring in them as one month of pregnancy flowered into the next. I felt the mystery in their muffled movements against the palms of my hands. I pressed my ear to the thin, taut barrier between us, listening for messages from an unfathomable reality I knew even then would forever alter mine.

A father is born to his children as surely as they are born to him.

I was 27 when the first one was en route, and not entirely sure I was ready for all this. In retrospect, I clearly was. My education was complete, my military service out of the way. I had acceptable work. I'd been married five years, and my wife and I had lived in Europe and a couple of places in the United States. Life, whose ticking my ears were becoming increasingly attuned to, seemed ready for more content.

The girls came three years apart. Like all small kids, they were implacably demanding and immobilizing. Rich fare for the appetite of a born worrier. I was near to bursting with love for them. The days when they were infants and small children were the most beatific of my life. I seemed to love devoid of self.

Ah, time. My daughters are teenagers now, noisily packing their psychological luggage for the great separation from us. These days, I seem to be a rather abstract contributor to their well-being; financier, consultant, enforcer of curfews and driving standards. Bath-giver, snuggler, storyteller no more, I feel my ego seeping into my dealings with them.

My daughters have the Big Plans of the young. They want to go away to college, travel abroad, become wealthy and sophisticated, help humanity, have deep friendships and great loves. They press inexorably toward the world outside my walls as they once pressed toward the light outside the womb. The older one goes off to study next year.

All of which brings me to the question, prompted by the passage last week of a state law requiring unmarried minors to get parental or judicial consent for abortions: What would I do if one of them became pregnant now?

The memory of my daughters before I knew they were daughters much colors my thinking about fetuses and abortion. The embryonic adults I see before my eyes now, however, tint my thoughts about women's sovereignty over their own lives.

I have never known an imperative as powerful as my daughters, and likely won't again. As sentimental as I am about infants and as much as I rather like the thought of myself as a grandfather someday, I do not think I could prefer any prospective person over the extant reality of my daughters. Please God the issue doesn't come up late, when there is more than an aggregation of undifferentiated cells at stake.

An abortion would be a trauma for us all.

But, require my daughters to turn from their hopeful destinations after but a few steps on the path? Burden them with the regrets of either giving up an infant like the kind I welcomed into my home or of taking on parenthood while the child in themselves still requires tending? Condemn them to a premature maturity?

Not me. Not my babies.

Sorry, Mom

Rampaging son-guilt on the morning after You-Know-Whose Day:
Apologies, Mom. Apologies and more apologies.

Apologies, to begin with, for cooping you up in that little hospital so
loaded with postwar neonatals, the nurses had to keep some of us in
sterilized dresser drawers.

And for all the trouble during toilet-training, all those sneaky trips
behind chairs long after you thought you'd won the battle.

For having made you cry by refusing to hug you the night you
returned home from the hospital with newborn Tommy when I was a
year old.

Apologies also for my raucous, childhood-long fight with Tom, which
was the bane of your motherhood. (Honest, Mom. Most of the time it
was his fault.)

Apologies especially for that momentous row that provoked you to
snatch away the new football we'd been shrilly fighting over all day,
carry it off into the kitchen and stab it with a paring knife, thereby
settling the matter.

And for the Easter chicks. I had no idea they'd grow out of their pink-
and-blue dye and turn into real chickens with big feet, scrabbling and
squawking all over your dining room floor. Did Dad really take them
"out to a farm"?

Apologies, too, for the dime-store turtles that escaped their shoe box each night, and had to be hunted down by you in the morning after we went off to school. Particularly sorry about the one you accidentally stepped on in the dark.

And for the small earthquakes Tom and I made when we'd shove the dining room table aside and play tackle football on the floor those evenings Dad wasn't home and you despaired of enforcing the rules.

Oh, yes, and for the time when, in utter frustration, you broke the plastic cereal bowl over my head after I laughingly taunted you for being too little to discipline me anymore. (It didn't hurt, Mom; it didn't even make me stop laughing. Besides, I had it coming, although not as much as Tommy did.)

Great, big, embarrassed apologies for that bout of hypochondria in sixth grade, when I was sure I had cancer and lay in bed, grief-stricken and moaning. Thanks for having Dr. Cunningham come to examine me and assure me there was nothing wrong at all. Apologies for having whimpered, as soon as he left the room, "Even doctors can be wrong."

Apologies for insisting as a high school freshman that you iron creases into my jeans. And thanks for finally insisting, in exasperation, that I learn to iron my own. Haven't often had creases in my jeans since.

Apologies, in fact, for my entire teenagerhood. For the pants you had to take up, then let down because their length never seemed just right to me. For the heaps of sodden towels I left in the aftermath of my 45-minute showers.

Apologies especially for the sleeplessness that has been your lot since we came along, and that prompted all those quiet nocturnal rounds to look in on us as we slept, even after we were nearly the size of men.

Apologies, Mom, for not going to church much anymore. Appreciate your prayers for my soul, and fervently hope they work.

Apologies, the biggest of all, for not being as single-mindedly devoted a parent to your grandchildren as you were to their father.

Last but not least, apologies for giving you apologies, instead of a new car or an ocean cruise for Mother's Day.

And apologies for being a day late, too.

My Life as a Dad

Extra tickle of poignancy this Father's Day — last one with older chick still in nest.

In a few months, she's out of here, gone to college, gone to found new generations of family debt. Free at last.

Authority lines inside old coop never be the same.

Enforce curfews? Stay up late at night to make sure she gets home OK? Critique eating habits, clothes, haircuts, grammar?

Not much longer.

Discreetly try to divine the particulars of her, uh, sexual ... uh ... (someone please provide soothing noun here)?

Well, rather not think a lot about that just now. Loaded her down to the axles with good advice on subject. Can only hope she won't dump it on side of road.

Clearly, am reaching endgame of fathering. First kid about to be unborn to me. Unborn into adulthood. Three more years and, pfffft, younger one unborn, too.

Touch of pre-un-partum depression maybe. Pretty soon, no one around to father. Stringy-crawed rooster strutting about with no chicks underfoot. Still crowing instructively, but no ears listening or pretending to.

(Still be borrowing my car, though, I bet.)

Appropriate time, perhaps, to reflect.

As father, I'm glad I:

■ Nuzzled, squeezed, tickled, tweaked, puppeteered, made funny sounds, etc., while they were little enough to be interested. Now, of course, distant. Womanly. Whole glee club of cartoon voices muffled, bursting to speak.

■ Plunged into stickiest of child-care chores, however genderly untraditional. Changed diapers, gave baths, Q-tipped skin folds. Administered Kaopectate, rectal thermometers, toenail clippers. Full-frontal fatherhood. After cleaning remnants of infant bowel episode from under fingernails, knew could handle anything short of brain surgery.

■ Read to them a lot. Even when tired. Even when distracted, depressed, tipsy (father, not kids). Even when wishing could strangle Seuss character for 12 millionth statement he does not like green eggs and ham. Rooster and warm chicks in warm embrace of story. Ah. Catch them reading sometimes even now. Inner lives on way. Revenge of the dad.

■ Waged fierce anti-television campaign. Restricted viewing time. Denounced entire idiot-making industry at every opportunity. Snarled about mouth-breathing whenever found them hooked up to Nintendo. Didn't work, but definitely old college try.

As father, I wish I'd:

■ Taught them better the value of money. Could still buy them some books on it probably. Little short of cash right now, though.

■ Shown them how to watch birds, identify flowers, hike, wilderness-camp, so they don't go through life afraid of spiders and uncomfortable about body functions when not in presence of ceramic tile. (Of course, would have to have learned all that myself; big hassle.)

■ Given them thinner thighs. Nothing wrong with ones they got, but would have at least forced teen-girl self-criticism into more meaningful directions.

■ Made them keep taking flute and violin lessons till age 18, despite tears, tantrums, threats of domestic terrorism. Hoped to fortify them with Mozart against Lenny Kravitz, Deee-lite and Siouxsie and the Banshees. Did hear older one sneak Respighi recording up to room once. Maybe small moral victory scored here despite apparent rout. Also, still time for younger one to be unborn into opera singer. Maybe not too late. Maybe can still influence her to ...

Influence. Ha!

Lights flashing, klaxon sounding ooo-ga, ooo-ga: WARNING — Major Role Change on Horizon.

Can handle it.

He says.

The Father of All Fears

According to a Parade Magazine poll this week, two-thirds of teenage boys have had sex, which is unsettling news to a father of teenage girls.

I doubt there's a more profound ambivalence than a father's toward the sexuality of his adolescent daughters.

There's a ton of irony in this. A father plays a determining role in his girls' eventual development into sexually capable beings, young women with high regard for themselves and a capacity for affection and intimacy with men. He is his daughters' first, innocent lover. His cuddling and stroking and twirling their hair around his finger during bottle-feeding and "Sesame Street" presage the young men who await them for the mating dance in the unimaginable future.

Things change as they get older, of course. He is more tentative and judicious about his hugs as he comes to feel the incipient form of a woman in his arms. But his affectionate relationship with them becomes a special point of pride as it endures the inevitable bad weather systems that sweep through the teen years. Not for him the destructive contentiousness of uncomprehending father and defiant daughter.

Then one Saturday evening there is a caller at the door.

It is Don Giovanni, tickling his mandolin and crooning, *"Deh! vieni alla finestra,"* and slyly anticipating his next conquest.

Only with difficulty is a father able to discern the figure of a 16-year-old boy with moussed hair drooping over his forehead, his weight shifting from one penny loafer to the other.

Because he is enlightened and has faith in his daughter's judgment, he greets the boy with a smile, like a fellow man. But the handshake he gives him is extra firm and carries a subliminal message: "Feel the strength, kid." Almost despite himself, he implants the subtle notion that he is a threat, even if he can't be there in the backseat of the car. It is the hapless, unsaid blessing he sends her off with.

What does he fear, exactly?

That she will become prematurely pregnant, certainly, and her youth will thus collapse instantly, no matter how the situation is resolved.

That she will contract disease.

That she will expose herself to an irremediable heartbreak because she invested herself before having attained a mature assessment of her great worth.

That she will become soured from having started too soon.

That she will become the love slave of a callow, pouting boy (but, a father wonders, is sex so powerful it can turn her mindlessly obedient after years of admonishing have failed to make her stop discarding clothes on the floor?).

Lastly, that — face it — she will learn, before he is altogether ready for her to, that there is male love more compelling than his.

A father must let go. Lay down a few theoretical rules, hope they have some force out there in the vibrant adolescent night, release her to begin her journey in strange lands.

So long as the trek leads back to his door by 11:30.

Parent Gap

In addition to all the other gaps in our demography — the '60s generation vs. their parents, early baby boomers vs. late baby boomers, all baby boomers vs. post-baby boomers — I've just uncovered another:

Parents in their 40s with teenage and young adult children vs. parents in their 40s with only small children.

As a person in the first category, I'm increasingly conscious of the differences between us and them.

It's shocking to me how out of date I already am as a raiser of young children. The children's books which I and child-rearers of my day could fairly chant in unison have been utterly superseded. "Sesame Street" has grown unfamiliar characters. My enthusiastic passing on of toys and games that delighted my daughters 10 and 15 years ago is met by the sort of politeness usually reserved for the well-intentioned elderly. Although clearly still within shouting distance of young manhood — clearly! — I'm starting to feel like a bloody grandparent around other people's small children.

Those in my age group who begat amid the tocking din of biological clocks running down are different from us who did so in the blush of youth.

For one thing, they videotape everything, beginning with the dilation of the cervix. Their kids' childhoods are destined to become TV miniseries, complete with cute titles ("The Dawn of Dawn" ... "Dawn in Play Group: The Adventure in Socialization Begins").

For another, they're more likely to anguish over getting their kids into the "right" kindergartens, lest they be shouldered off the Harvard track before they've learned cursive.

Of course, almost all new parents consider their tykes precious. It's just that old new parents, by virtue of their superior knowledge of how the world works, tend to go to greater lengths to control kids' environments and maximize their opportunities.

We early breeders hadn't figured out a lot about our own lives yet and tended to be a little dumber. We more or less assumed nature and common sense would get us through OK. Our kids probably had a little less pressure on them, but a somewhat smaller percentage may qualify for med school.

I'm not sure which group does a better job overall. Younger parents may be a tad better for little kids, more energetic and patient.

Older parents, however, may be better for teens. Younger parents of teens tend to think of themselves as not all that far removed from their own teen years and can thus be a little too cocksure and over-reactive. Older parents of teens may be less alarmist, less interventionist, more commonsensical.

I miss having little kids of my own; miss their unabashed delights and soothable pains. Being the young father of small children was my finest hour, because my most unselfish.

But I'm different now. I don't have the patience I used to around small kids. I take umbrage at their tantrums. I don't miss sponging spit-up off the carpets or standing in drizzles watching 6-year-olds play herd-style soccer.

On balance, I'm glad I jumped into the river of biological progression farther upstream, and rather chuckle at the thought of a father in his 50s contending with the intricate demands of Indian Princesses.

They really should put a statute of limitations on Indian Princesses.

The Gift of Children

Nah, that's OK. We don't want anything for Father's Day. Don't need any ties. Got plenty of socks. Have hardly had the chance to wear the stuff from last year.

All we want is for you to be straight and true, competent at life and capable of love, OK? That's enough for us.

This may come as a mild shock to you as you prepare to fawn over us Sunday, but we haven't always defined ourselves primarily as your fathers. We've never entirely given up on ourselves as some pretty striking dudes. Even now, there are times when we muse on what lives we might have led, what places we might have seen, what deeds we might have done, if we'd chosen not to have you. Sometimes we speculate about what women instead of your mothers might have become our mates.

But all such thoughts are ultimately unconvincing, because they negate the possibility of you. You are a mountain range on our emotional landscape. It's impossible to imagine the vista without you.

There's a lot of propaganda about fathers. You can blame the greeting-card industry for much of it, but part of the responsibility belongs on our doorstep. Our instinct has been to show you only our good sides — virtuous, patient, law-upholding. You'd be surprised how many times we've put on righteous demeanors like ill-fitting clothes to get you to do the right thing. You aren't very old when you begin to see through us. But that's fine. You have a right to know us, sooner or later, as the adults we really are. People who don't have all the answers; who get fearful, play hunches, hope for the best.

The time will come, if it hasn't already, when our roles reverse and you are the ones who must decide how we will be cared for. Then it will be your turn to play-act.

What do you owe us? A lot, according to the propaganda. Not much, many of us are inclined to think.

All we did was follow a natural imperative, make a minimal physical input. ("Accessories to reproduction," as one of John Updike's Eastwick witches referred to us.) Unlike your mothers, whose very bodies changed to accommodate the fact of your existence, we — most of us — just kind of hung around, helping deal with whatever came up after your births. We had to earn our relevance every day.

We got a heck of a lot out of it, though.

Men take a long time to understand love, and you helped us know it in its fullest dimension. Beatific we felt as we held you in our arms when you were small. Wonderstruck that we could have done so well as to help make you. Rousing ourselves to care for you has been, for most of us, easy as pie.

Don't get us wrong. We'll take whatever credit you want to give. But never underestimate what a snap it's been to love you.

All right. If it makes you feel good to give us a little something Sunday, go ahead. There is that polo shirt we've had an eye on. That bright cotton sweater. They are the sorts of things we've bought our fathers on Father's Day, after all. Wouldn't be right to deny you the outlet.

Having been sons, we know fathers eventually recede from children's lives; must, if kids are to become independent adults.

So deck us out in finery for our big fade, and don't feel a lot of guilt about it.

Sweater or no, we have a lot to say thanks for.

Gone with the Tide

Come on. Don't let that weedy sea of sentimentality breach the wall. Finger firmly in the dike, now.

There's a good parent.

Keep reminding yourself that every year thousands of people — millions — cart their first-borns off to college for the first time. This is not blazing a trail. This is bumping along in a deeply worn rut, however unfamiliar to you.

Think precedence. Take heart.

Besides, it's not as though the kid hadn't been practically drooling on the floors in anticipation of trading the nest for a place of real freedom.

And it's not as though you, dike-finger, hadn't muttered over her adult-like comings and goings, "Yes, it probably is time for her to leave."

Motoring west in a borrowed minivan loaded to the gunwales with plastic crates and garbage bags of cosmetics, audiotapes, eccentric clothing, your lips are sealed. Inside, however, you keep marveling over the realization, burgeoning with each mile that whisks beneath the tires, that she is history, she is out of here, she will never truly live with us again.

She, meantime, seems to be handling the momentous transformation with aplomb — stretched on a rear seat, covered with your raincoat, sleeping the drowned sleep of infants and the college-aged.

Clearly, this is no time for unhelpful analogies. Those memories of infant carriers strapped into back seats; of babes with drooped and sleep-heated cheeks and yesteryear's car, long since junked, smelted, probably part of a refrigerator somewhere, ticking toward the grandparents' place — who needs them just now?

It was challenge enough sifting the chaos of her room for transportable items. Placing hands on childhood mementos, hearing judgment passed (some of them sentenced to being left behind, to life without parole). A person had to be practical, was all. Hard-headed. Stout-fingered, dike-wise. Take Ralph the stuffed raccoon, dilapidated from long bedfellowship, and wedge him between stereo components to keep them from banging against the side of the packing box.

At the college, the official welcomers try to caress your stoically encapsulated discomforts. We understand, they say. We know. Eighteen-year-wide holes are what you're staring into.

The parental units cling to every word.

The freshmen move their heads in slow swivels, scanning the possibilities, one another.

In the dorm room, which is more than a little knocked-about looking, are the roommate and the roommate's parents. There is also a great deal of resolute cheeriness, routing of extension cords, looking for things to say and be busy with.

Sticking around is what it really is.

Then, down in the dormitory parlor, excuses for lingering exhausted, there are hugs. You squeeze the back of her neck, slip her a couple of extra twenties. You say, with a fervor that surprises even you, "If there's anything you need, just let me know. Anything. I don't care what."

Confidence, self-regard, brilliance, a fruitful, happy, star-blessed life — just say the word.

The van is lighter on the drive home.

And now you are feeling very much a dweller of the lowlands. On the other hand, you get to unstick her audiotapes of bizarrely named musical groups from between the seat cushions of the car and reset the stereo buttons for classical, public and oldies radio. Your wheels again. Consolation prize.

Clearly, this is no time to be unrealistic. The entire point, after all, was always to unleash a functioning human being on the world. This was never a still photo. It was from the start a film, a longitudinal study.

Besides, the sea change will be gotten used to. There will be ebb tide, and finger can be withdrawn from dike.

Besides, there's still one at home for a few more years.

Tick, tick, tick.

Touching Base

Like inheriting freckles or being dropped on your head as an infant, the Major League baseball team of your childhood has a lifelong effect.

I am afflicted in this way by the Pittsburgh Pirates. A decade in Detroit has converted my heart to the Tigers, but my viscera still belong to the Bucs.

Visiting home last weekend, I went to my first Pirates game in several years. I took my father with me, for what could be more evocative of an earlier innocence than going with your dad to watch the team you prayed to as a kid take on the hated Cincinnati Reds?

My father is 73 and long retired from the steel mill. Having come through a triple heart bypass, he's ready for some good, strong late innings. He and I had not been to a Pirates game together since I was 11.

We packed a small cooler with beer and snacks, fired up his land yacht of a 1983 Olds and headed for P-burgh, 35 miles away.

Not, unfortunately, for Forbes Field. That holy venue had long since succumbed to a high, hard fastball — the wrecker's. Our destination was the great expressway-girdled concrete bowl of Three Rivers Stadium.

We arrived early and sat for a time on a log at the edge of the parking lot, sipping cans of Iron City. My father tipped the white "DeFrank and Son Body Shop" baseball cap back on his head and conjured the streetcar rides to Forbes Field. He conjured the taverns that spilled the smells of bratwurst and anticipation onto the crowded sidewalks around the old stadium.

Traffic on elevated freeway ramps whooshed high above us, all around.

Our stadium seats turned out to be in nosebleed territory. Below were spread the glories of a modern ballpark: expansive shock of kelly green artificial turf; hot orange, mustard yellow and cherry red seats; royal blue fences. Hard to imagine memories would stick to these antiseptic surfaces the way they stuck to the wood and iron of Forbes Field.

Three Rivers had all the teases. Rock music blared between batters. The scoreboard ceaselessly egged fans on to clap, whistle, dance.

The game turned out to be a meticulous pitchers' duel, which created vast human silences not even the scoreboard could dispel.

All was not what I'd have wished.

Eventually, my father and I began to fill the silences. We loosened up and started throwing the baseball talk. The thing about talking baseball talk is that you are seldom provably wrong. When you are, it's never held against you.

Our unease with cartoon colors and inch-high players began to ebb. My father invoked the names of Pirates past, great and obscure. Pittsburgh was his boyhood team, too. By the seventh, we were singing "Take Me Out to the Ballgame" with stirring abandon.

Late in the scoreless game, I said, in baseball talk, "Looks like it may take Dr. Longball to win this one."

But this one was won by Mr. Pop-up Bunt, which a Pirates relief pitcher flubbed, opening a 6-run Reds ninth.

We took the 6-1 loss in stride, my father and I.

Later, we were at the log again, into the Iron City and the roasted peanuts. Around us, great knots of traffic tried to dissolve. We felt a little conspicuous, slightly delinquent, very pleased.

"You know," my father said, "those seats, they weren't so bad after all."

Death in the Balance

Two weeks ago this morning, I was driving south on I-75 en route to my hometown to visit my father, who'd just been hospitalized after a particularly bad night.

My father didn't have much time left. I knew that. Prostate cancer had run amok through his bones and turned an active retirement into a painful, sleepless pantomime. The female hormones he took as therapy had made pale dough of his dark, supple body. Fine hair had spouted incongruously on his bald head. I'd given him another month or two to live.

What I didn't know, motoring along somewhere between the Rouge River Bridge and the Flat Rock Mazda plant, was that he was already gone. He died, by my later reckoning, when I'd been on the road about 30 minutes and had a good 4½ hours of highway ahead of me.

When I got to the hospital lobby, I asked the woman at the information desk for his room number. She punched a few keys on her computer, and a directory of patients whose last names began with "R" stacked itself on her screen.

The screen was set at an oblique angle to me, but I could make out the glowing green letters a third of the way down the list:

Ricci, Ralph P. ... EXPIRED.

The woman's face went ashen.

"He's dead, isn't he?" I said, a feeling much like wonder blossoming in my chest.

She looked at me. "I am so sorry."

My father had suffered his first heart attack when he was my age, 45. Many times over the next three decades, I'd wondered how I'd learn of his death. I'd have bet on a warbling telephone in the middle of the night, a voice on the other end choking with the news. Computer directory was a possibility I'd not considered.

His death raised a week-long tide of clan gathering, funeral home visitation, necktie wearing, hugging, consoling, overeating. I experienced a kind of swamping internally, too. I still haven't inventoried the flotsam of feelings cast off by the sudden absence of this most central man in my life; my enduring notion of manhood; a figure I'd been in flight from or in return to almost constantly since adolescence.

So far, what I feel most noticeably is a lowness of spirits. More dramatic emotions no doubt lurk beneath the surface, however, waiting for this early numbness to ebb.

I strain to recall the meticulous man who rubbed my pitching arm with liniment after Little League games, taught me to drive, cosigned a bank note when I was 19 so I could go off alone to work a summer in Europe (even though it mystified him that I would embrace such loneliness). That man has been temporarily subsumed by the melancholy figure who trudged through the final illness.

So I wait for the waters to abate and the long mopping-up operation called grieving to properly begin. Meantime, my thoughts keep turning to a small irony.

In 1987, immediately after my father underwent heart bypass surgery, his newly implanted pacemaker misfired and plunged him into crisis. In the waiting room, my mother and sister clung to a determined optimism. Reading the grim faces of the surgeons, however, I concluded he was as good as dead. I went off to be alone, to wrestle myself into accepting this stunning reality. I was unaware, and would be for several hours, that my father had already begun a slow climb back from the edge.

Perhaps you see the parallel. For a time in 1987 my father was dead for me alone. Anointed, embalmed and buried, with me his sole mourner. And then, during that drive two Sundays ago, when I was the only member of the family unreachable with the bad news, I'd pictured him in the hospital — not happy to be there, but relieved, afloat on a merciful vapor of morphine, awaiting my arrival. For those 4½ hours he was alive for me alone.

It seems to me now a balancing of accounts, and I take a certain comfort in that.

Empty Places

In the memory room, Son sits amid knickknacks, bowling trophies, stacks of crossword puzzles. Dead eye of old TV, switched off, color of overaged pea soup, stares him right in face. Seiko wall clock, gift of Son few years back (no one buys Japanese in this town), confides, "tsk."

Shelves, tables crowded with framed photos. Clear plastic banners stuck with snapshots hang from walls.

Theme of photos is kids. Kids in baptismal dresses. In ponytails, Little League caps, gowns and mortarboards. Son's grandparents as kids. Son's parents as kids. Son and his brother and sister as kids. Son's own kids. Kids Son doesn't even recognize. (When Son and siblings stopped supplying, Son's parents turned to others. Memory room requires constant feeding.)

Dad dead two weeks now.

Not "gone," Son keeps reminding people. "Dead." Get used to idea. Face up. Son in very literal phase. Avoids violin of euphemism, dreads scratching up dance of sentiment.

Son flaunting lots of bravery and nonchalance these days. Gospel of "acceptance" frequently on his lips. Determinedly optimistic about Mom's future.

Mom, after 51½-year marriage, unconvinced. Embraces sneak attacks of sorrow — like sudden falls off cliffs — with widespread arms and ready tears. Fusses with documents of decedence. Keeps eye on diet. Says rosary. Tries to smile. Watches baseball on TV (colors all wrong since Dad go- ... dead). Ponders quiet, scented alone-ness called widowhood. Feels breakable.

Weird for Son to be alone at home with Mom. "Home," since 7:47 a.m., May 1, 1946 (Son's big debut), always Mom and Dad. Son can almost feel Mom striving to double output of essence to fill void. Feels chill of Dad's absence whenever her efforts flag.

Meantime, much to be done. Lawyers, insurance policies, bank accounts, pensions, Social Security (bureaucracies notably unskilled at grieving).

Mom writes checks for purchases long put off by expenditure-wary Dad. Says, "I hope Dad's not mad at me for spending money like this."

Ruthlessly rational Son, heatedly: "You're boss now. Your money. Do whatever you wish."

Secretly humbled by how much they were one.

Son plays master of house. Sells Dad's old Oldsmobile tad too cheap. Terrible salesman (just ask Mom). Mows lawn per posthumous instructions. Installs double dead bolt in basement door (security a new priority).

Botches laying of rubber treads on basement stairs (no one around if she slips and falls). In solitude of spick-and-span basement, experiences major sob at thought of how Dad, tidiest of men, would have done it. No air bubbles. No errant smears of Liquid Nails.

On Labor Day, fixes cookout-for-two, takes Mom to cemetery.

Dad high on outside wall of double vaults overlooking green valley, near brother and best friend. "Dad always loved being outside," Mom says.

Son elevates on tiptoes and raps speckled red marble facade. Sound is hollow. Room, he realizes, for her.

Sitting in memory room, Seiko ticking off minutes, Son mulls double vault filled to capacity. Thinks, where is home then?

Birthday Wishes

He'd have been 75 yesterday, Jan. 6, the Epiphany, "the Feast of the Three Wise Guys," as he liked to say.

He could be quite a wise guy himself, my old man. Despite his moodiness (twang on, strands of DNA) he rarely tired of leg-pulling, especially where his grandkids were concerned. "This is my goofy Grandpa," is how my younger daughter used to introduce him to her playmates when she was small.

Wise, goofy — take your pick. Or, I should say, pick your moment. Since his death not quite five months ago, I've thought more than once of a moment several years past when I asked him how old he thought he'd live to be. My father searched his wisdom and said, "Oh, I'd guess 75."

I did not much care for his figure. He'd just come through triple-bypass heart surgery, and was, for the first time in a quarter-century, free of debilitating angina. He was golfing, washing cars, mowing lawns, staying out late with old friends. At 70, he proclaimed he was having the time of his life.

"Come on, Dad," I told him, "there's no reason now you can't make it to 85 or even 90. You're just afraid of pressing your luck if you talk cocky. You're low-balling, and you know it." He shrugged. He was basing his answer, he said, on something quite concrete: His parents had died at about age 75. How well a person happened to feel at the moment was a feather in the wind compared to that weighty statistic.

And then a year and a half ago, prostate cancer sprang an ambush. Last Aug. 18, it carried him off, 111 days shy of 75.

Back when we discussed how long he thought he'd live, he'd seemed to me remarkably serene about his estimate. There was little serenity, however, when the end actually drew near. He was afraid, and, gentled by the terminal-stage morphine, as dependent as a child on my mother, who cared for him at home until only a few hours before he died. His strong religious faith did not seem to ease his passage much (so far, I've known no one whose belief in an afterlife made it easier to accept his or her own death. As my father, wise guy, liked to say, "Everybody wants to go to heaven, but nobody wants to die").

Recently, I spent some time with my mother to help her (and me) through the first holidays without him. He loved Christmas. He couldn't get enough of its sentimentality and festivity.

His absence in my parents' house is still breathtaking. Around every corner, he is amazingly not there. My mother battles daily to domesticate this wild animal of loss. For long periods it will lie peacefully at her feet, then leap without warning to bury claws in her heart.

So, yesterday, a birthday but no birthday boy.

People who know grieving say it helps to get through an entire year. They say it takes a year of stumbling over the special days — the lost one's birthday and wedding anniversary, the first incomplete Christmas, the first conspicuously unresurrectional Easter, the first too-independent Independence Day, etc.

Meantime, a person takes some comfort in fine, worn adages: The dead live on in the good they've done others. Love for a life doesn't end merely because the life has.

Happy birthday, dear old wise guy. I won't stop keeping track.

A CERTAIN
SEASON

CHAPTER TWO

Tremors of Spring

Vicky Johnston poked two fingers into the soil, some of it still frozen, some already a brown soup for half a centimeter's depth. She cleared away dead leaf litter and parted the khaki duff of last year's ground cover, then looked up, smiling.

"Here," she said. "Look here."

She lifted the tip of a bright green blade of infant grass. New. This year's.

"The sun has warmed this spot just enough to give these little shoots a start," she said.

It is enough for me. I am calling it spring.

Earlier this week, in the midst of that three-day cold snap, an inner tremor seemed to be indicating the season had changed. It's hard to get a precise seismic reading of such things in the workaday world. I decided to drive to Canada's Point Pelee National Park to see if I could tune it in better, and to look for physical evidence.

Snow was scarce on the brown, ironed-flat fields of Essex County during the drive. It had retreated to the ditches along the road, or been stranded on frozen farm ponds. Here and there, thawing earth bled water onto the edges of the pavement.

The sky was cloudless, and the light had a kind of blue ripeness to it. At late morning the sun was high in its dome; its rays seeped into the car from all angles, suffusing everything in unwintry warmth.

At Point Pelee, that stiletto thrust into Lake Erie, the air was plenty cold. But it was the light, not the air, that bore spring, naturalist Johnston said as we walked one of the park's woodland trails.

Liberated from a low wintertime aspect, the sun has begun its climb to dominance, expanding the daytime. Migratory birds, stirred by the longer periods of light, are just beginning the urgent northward journey to their breeding grounds. Red-winged blackbirds and American robins have been in evidence at the Point for a week; tundra swans have been sighted.

"And this morning, from my bedroom window, I heard a song sparrow," Johnston said. "When you hear it, you know spring is on the way; it is one of the earliest to come back."

A few moments later, a song sparrow sang its irregular song in the distance west of the trail. It sounded like a flute being playfully warmed up.

A person didn't have to strain the senses, Johnston pointed out, to know. "You need only stand facing the light and feel it on your cheeks and forehead, and even with your eyes closed and your ears plugged, you can feel spring."

The place where she uncovered the new season's grass was about 50 yards from the east beach, in the forested interior of the peninsula. At the water's edge, there was no question which season ruled.

An imperious northeast wind scoured the shore, pushing ice floes through open blue water toward Ohio, stinging flesh to numbness. With its disorderly piles of ice shards, the beach was the last place the new season would appear, Johnston said.

Thus does spring, like love, begin in inner, protected places.

Such as within us. We are more reliable indicators than calendars, mean temperatures and the position of the sun over the tropics.

When the geological plates of attitude shift and release that unmistakable new optimism, openness, buoyancy, winter is done. Anyone else feeling the earthquake?

Hill 255

The place where they died, a man-made hill scrubbed by wind and bordered by rushing traffic, is inhospitable to a sense of peace.

Giant trucks roar ceaselessly on Middlebelt Road as they position themselves to get on I-94. Jets shriek and whine overhead: huge, straining, grotesquely slowed, showing dirty underbellies as they sink toward the runway at Detroit Metro.

Two years ago, you could not get near here. The shattered remains of Northwest Airlines Flight 255 lay down below on Middlebelt. In the dancing light of emergency vehicles, yellow body blankets grew like great, sad dandelions on this hill.

Peaceful or not, it is a place where the human need to remember toils against the instinct to forget.

On Monday afternoon, a relentless sun bore down on the hill and the stone marker that reads simply "255." A dozen memorial displays huddled around it:

An empty, hand-painted bottle of Perrier-Jouet Fleur de Champagne 1983. Nine American flags lolling in plastic cones pushed into the earth, or, having been tipped by the relentless wind, fidgeting on the ground. A dried twig wreath with the word, "Mel," and figures of an Indian, a pheasant, a jet plane. A weathered styrofoam heart saying "Laura."

One of the displays was a coffee mug bearing the name "Pat." It was weighted with rocks and planted in silk tulips. Attached, inside a clear plastic Ziploc bag, was a handwritten poem, signed by "J.K.G.," and dated 6-18-89. It read, in part,

So special a man
So vital a part of all our yesterdays
And still our tomorrows.
In our hearts you remain,
giving courage and strength
To face our sorrows.

The hill had been newly mowed and swept of debris — gotten ready for remembering — in anticipation of tonight's 7:30 service honoring the 156 who perished here. Forty-two bright orange bags of grass clippings were piled against the I-94 East sign, waiting to be picked up by highway crews.

A young man parked his pickup next to the bags and walked up the hill carrying a display of red and white carnations on a spindly tripod. He sank the legs deep into the earth and stood silently for a few moments, the wind playing havoc with his hair.

He works nearby, he said, and the planes pass so close above he can look up and see passengers at the windows. He'd been there the night 255 had gone down, and rubble and flame are imprinted on his memory.

The carnations, which cost $36, were his way "to pay respect." He resents, he said, the way the media "turn this into a zoo once a year" in their efforts to provoke remembering. He will go to the memorial service tonight, and try to ignore all the cameras.

We have digested Flight 255. The thought of it no longer leaves us breathless. Loved ones' lives have begun to knit around the holes left by the tragedy. There have been 750,000 takeoffs and landings at Metro since.

"Life," wrote Joseph Conrad, "closes over a sorrow the way the sea closes over a dead body, no matter how much love has gone to the bottom."

But that is not the same as forgetting. Forgetfulness will be a long time taking this hill.

Taking a Bath in the Pool

I don't want anyone to get the idea that there's an NCAA basketball tournament betting pool at my office, or that I'd have anything to do with it if there were.

That would be illegal, and, like Richard Nixon, I can assure you I am hardly ever a crook.

But, just for the heck of it, let's say someone at the Free Press — somebody, say, down amid the boilers and hissing steam pipes of the sports department — put together such a pool. Let's say he or she circulated copies of blank tournament-bracket forms around the building and invited others to fill them in and return them with $5 apiece.

Further, let's say so many people signed up — from grand seigneurs of the editor ruling class to tattered wretches on the politics beat — that the first prize swelled to more than $480.

Since we're blue-skying here, let's also say that when the pool standings were posted after the first day of play, two people stood atop the squirming pile with records of 15-1.

Let's say one of them was, oh, a columnist. We'll call him "Jim."

OK, let's say that last Friday, after the 32 games of the complete first round had been played, this "Jim" person had correctly predicted the winners of 26.

Well, even if you are among the approximately 4 percent of the population not currently involved in such a pool, you can probably imagine how he would have reacted.

You would expect him to have walked about with smug, half-closed eyes, flaunting his discernment and sunning in the envy of colleagues near-smothered in the middle of the pile.

And you would probably be right.

He might even have begun counting out his winnings in his mind, amusing himself with thoughts of a surprise $50 bill left overnight on the bookbags of each of his two teenage kids. If this person had any such kids, that is.

Here's what would really be funny, though. What if this "Jim" character, after much eager anticipation, sat down in front of his TV last weekend and watched as one after another of his picks toppled into the dust during the tournament's second round? Oklahoma beaten by North Carolina. Michigan ravaged by Loyola Marymount. Mighty Louisville humbled by a university named after a canning jar (Ball State).

Not only that, but suppose he found himself unable to enjoy even games whose outcomes he'd correctly predicted. Instead of rooting for teams he wanted deep down in his soul to win, he sat mutely hoping for victory by teams he had a financial interest in. Suppose he could not even cheer on dear old Ohio State (where, just to make things ironical, let's say he'd once been a student) against University of Nevada, Las Vegas, which he sincerely hated but had picked to win the entire tournament.

You can see the painful contradictions in this.

At any rate, when last Monday came, this "Jim" would have been far from the strutting peacock of a few days before. A chicken, more like it, plucked of his conceit and tied for 10th place with 14 other people in the office pool. If it existed.

The prospect of five hundred easy bucks? *Pfft.* Gone like a spritz of cologne in a windstorm.

All he'd stand to win now was a consolation prize: This weekend, he can shake his fist at the TV and cry, "Die, UNLV, die!" and mean it from the bottom of his heart.

Going for the Burn

My friend Smitty swore it was going to be a piece of cake, "like mowing your lawn for six hours. Grandmothers in flip-flops do it."

The part about closed-head injuries didn't come up till much later.

So, sure, I signed up to participate in my first triathlon.

Unlike the usual triathlon, which consists of swimming, running and bicycling, the Maumee Valley Triathlon was made up of a 9-mile canoe race, a 9-mile hike with 20 percent of one's weight on one's back and a 25-mile bike race. A kind of a plodder's triathlon. Right up my alley.

Ordinarily, I don't do any of those things. I'd never backpacked, unless you count those forced marches in the Army. I'd been in a canoe only twice, and on a bike maybe three times in the past five years.

Naturally, I didn't bother to train for the event, except to not get enough sleep the night before (I had to help chaperon my daughter's eighth-grade dance party and didn't get to bed until after midnight). I was up before 5 a.m. and motoring toward Maumee, Ohio, bleary-eyed and filled with something I wouldn't describe as colossal eagerness.

When I arrived on the banks of the Maumee River, I didn't see any grandmothers. Unh-uh. Instead, I found myself among the Spandex People, that brightly clad, highly muscle-defined nation that emerges from the broader populace each weekend to set personal records, go for the burn and otherwise achieve corporally. The only participants of grandparenting age seemed to be Smitty and me.

Soon the two of us were on the river in our rented canoe, digging our paddles feverishly into the brown water. Trying to coordinate our strokes. Trying not to look at Smitty's watch. Being easily passed by smiling Spandex duos.

We blistered our hands and pushed our upper bodies to the absolute breaking point. At that juncture we were about one-third of the way through the canoe course.

Somehow, we pressed on. We began to think that there was no end to this canoe race, that we'd somehow landed in an episode of "The Twilight Zone," and our fate for all eternity was to strain in anguish on a murky river to nowhere. What a metaphor.

When the river exit site finally came into view, I'd have wept with joy if I'd had the energy.

Our packs awaited; mine weighed 34 pounds. Smitty had said to load it with something soft and compact. I'd pondered this for many days, and finally hit on the perfect load: a 25-pound sack of unbleached Gold Medal flour. With some bottles of water and extra clothing, I would carry it back up the shore of this river.

Forward we trudged. Some Spandex People ran past us with their packs. A bridge, one we'd passed beneath shortly after setting out in our canoe, would signal that the end of the hiking course was near. After two hours on foot, I could feel water squishing in a great blister on the ball of my left foot, but could find no trace of the desperately desired landmark. "They've moved the damned bridge," I said bitterly to Smitty. "They took it apart brick by brick and hauled it away."

But 25 minutes later we'd finished the hike and were on our bikes and, if I may be permitted a moment of unaccustomed immodesty, singularly kicking butt.

On my borrowed mountain bike, with Smitty dogging my rear wheel, I edged up to 24 miles an hour. The air beat gladly on my face. Young cornfields slid by on either side. Now, this was more like it.

This was also, unfortunately, when I lifted my right hand to rub sweat from my eyes and, in doing so, pushed the handlebars minutely too hard with my left. The mountain bike swooned beneath me, and I was suddenly in unassisted flight, performing a graceful, prolonged arabesque.

As the asphalt rose to meet me, I felt an idiot's calm. I turned my left shoulder to the pavement the way you turn in bed to a lover. Hard-hearted lover, this one.

My parts hit in this order: left hip, left elbow, left shoulder, head. Especially head. I won't soon forget the terrific smack of my helmet against the pavement. Oblivion lay just a few inches of plastic foam away.

After, I knelt in the grass along the cornfield for a while trying to reorder my senses. I'd hamburgered my elbow and knee. A lovely sack of fluids was forming on my hip. There was a tongue of brilliant garnet across my left shoulder, as though I'd been licked by a witch. Over and over I replayed the mental tape of my head hitting.

We finished the race, but grimly and against a stiffening wind that had us straining to maintain 9 miles an hour. I kept both hands on the handlebars no matter what flew into my eyes. Smitty rode ahead of me to part the wind and encouraged me to stay close to his rear wheel. I declined.

"I'm gun-shy about kissing the pavement again," I said.

"You didn't kiss the pavement," said Smitty, who'd seen my fall in his rearview mirror. "You had all-out sexual relations with it."

The rain began just as we pulled in to the finish line, six hours and 16 minutes after pushing off in the canoe.

Was it worth it?

Why, heck yes. I got a lot out of it.

I got a whole summer's worth of canoeing, backpacking and bicycling out of the way in one fell swoop.

I got a 25-pound sack of flour which I can eventually make pasta out of. Not just your ordinary pasta, but interesting, traveled pasta. Pasta with a past. I got one beaut of a trophy to show people I know well enough to drop my pants in front of. My entire left ham, from mid-buttock to knee, has gone the color of blueberries, with a spreading aurora of lemon-lime at the edges.

Last but not least, I got a new gewgaw for the old maxim shelf:

Anybody who bikes without a helmet is already brain-damaged.

Dream Machine

It's hard for someone who was lucky to get through high school physics to comprehend the significance of the information Voyager 2 has been beeping back from Neptune.

One thing is clear, however: You have got to love that ungainly little contraption.

For 12 years, Voyager 2 has been a real-life, interplanetary R2D2, game and loyal and obedient. Launched Aug. 20, 1977, and joined by its pal Voyager 1 two weeks later, it was originally intended to explore just Jupiter and Saturn. But then we asked it to trek a few billion miles farther to scope out Uranus and Neptune, and, true to its faithful nature, it radioed back, "Sure thing, boss."

Physically, Voyager 2 is an unlikely love object, a 12-foot dish atop a 6-foot, 10-sided box bristling with appendages and trailing a 43-foot antenna.

It is thoroughly unpretentious. Its two on-board computers have about four-tenths of 1 percent as much memory capacity as the typical personal computer of today.

It is soft-spoken. The signal we receive from it measures about ten-quadrillionth of a watt. It weighs about the same as a Toyota Tercel.

Oh, Voyager 2 has had a few mechanical hiccups. Seven months after launch, presumedly while still under warranty, one of its radio receivers blinked out. Then, while cruising Saturn in 1981, it threw a bearing in the movable platform on which its cameras are mounted.

But the fact remains, that baby has 4.4 billion miles on it and hasn't been in the shop once. Doesn't have a speck of rust, either.

In twelve years, Voyager has given us more information about the outer planets of the solar system than humankind had accumulated over the previous 450 millenia of its existence.

The cost to date has been $865 million, about the price of 1⅔ Stealth bombers. Or, think of it this way. Cleaning up after the pin-striped, big-money sweethearts who savaged the savings and loan industry is going to cost us 191 times more.

Voyager 2 is strictly pre-Reagan America. It was born of a philosophy completely at odds with that which has since trashed the national parks, glorified conspicuous consumption, starved the child development programs, tripled the national debt and generally encouraged the country to live as though there is no tomorrow.

Voyager 2 is an expression of an America that is patient, modest, intelligent, curious about the larger meaning of existence. Out there in the cold, black void 2.9 million miles from home, it is a glowing example of the rewards that come with taking care of the future.

Early this morning, the spacecraft took its last close look at anything in our solar system. From here on out, its destiny is sort of melancholy.

In 40,000 years, give or take a millenium, it will pass within about 10 trillion miles of the star Ross 248. About 256,000 years later it will cruise past the star Sirius at a distance of about 25 trillion miles. After that, it will wander, more or less endlessly, through The Milky Way.

Scientists think Voyager 2 will cross from our solar system into interstellar space in 20 or 30 years. Here's hoping they can fix the time more precisely, so we can all get out on our porches and wave a fond good-bye.

Harvest Dance

We have come to hear the whoosh of wind in the trees and the murmur of yellow jackets flitting near the juices flowing from the winepress.

We are here for the stemmy scent of the just-picked vignoles grapes and the resiny smell of new oak barrels that will receive the juice. For the sight of the winery's dogs lazing in the warm sun near the motorized crushing machine, and of the muddy, mint-colored soup that will settle out and ferment into clear gold wine.

We are here, in all, for the special music of the harvest and grape crush at the Seven Lakes Vineyard near Holly.

Unlike wine maker Chris Guest, we have not been obliged to dance all year long.

As farmer, Guest has had to let willful nature lead him around the floor. Sometimes it whisks him along so that his feet scarcely touch down, sometimes it grinds its heels into his insteps and sometimes it does both in the course of a single season's song.

Guest is a man of 36 with a perpetual look of bemusement and resignation on his face. Small wonder.

Last year the dance was a swift mazurka. The season was hot and dry and produced the ripest and most abundant harvest in the winery's nine-year history. This year it was a cool and rainy waltz. On Sept. 23, an early frost set in, stunning the vines before much of the vignoles had optimally ripened, and necessitating the immediate commencement of the harvest.

Then early last week a footsore and pessimistic Guest discovered he was saved. A section of the vineyard beset by the "noble rot," botrytis, which dries the grapes and concentrates their sugars, showed unprecedented ripeness. The grapes from this section could be blended with the greener fruit to make up for the latter's shortcomings.

And there was this little coda: Since the killing frost, the weather has been nearly perfect. "A little tease from God," the wine maker calls it.

Pilgrims have been coming to see Chris Guest almost from the day his first vine was planted. From the start there was something infectious about his enterprise. When he made his first wines at Seven Lakes, he seemed almost giddy from the whirl.

Over time, he planted more vines and refined his methods and saw his vignoles make it onto the prestigious wine list at the London Chop House in Detroit.

Yet the winery has only flirted with breaking even, and as it has expanded the dance has come to be fraught with greater and greater consequence.

"I was more into the fun back then," Guest says with a scant smile. "If you didn't have to depend on it for your living, it would be a heck of a lot of fun, but there's a lot of stress when you do this for your livelihood. It's a lot less sure business than a lot of other businesses. Much more depends on forces out of your control. I guess you can tell I'm not the same guy."

Dissonance buzzes in the air. Talk of payrolls and distribution problems — it does not compute for us.

Like the yellow jackets nosing at the crushed grapes in the winepress, we are visitors from another order of existence. Soon enough we'll be back among the contrivances of urban life, where the dance is a kind of lockstep and the music is hard to hear.

For one harvest afternoon we choose to be deafened by the romance of soil, weather and tradition that culminates in a bit of magic corked in a bottle. Our only request: Play on.

A Sweeping Metaphor

Fall, you know, is all about death. The end of baseball, the withering of annual flowers, etc.

I'm sorry, but that's our culture for you. I didn't invent it, I just try to work with it.

Most of us don't think much about death. For one thing, it really undermines a person's enthusiasm for chipping away at the old mortgage, and Lord knows the savings and loans are already in deep enough trouble.

When we do think of death, we tend to envision it as a sleepy passage to a kind of courtroom where a judge is going to review our rap sheets and send us either to a sunny land where the local sports teams always win or to a stuffy office where we'll spend eternity filling out IRS forms.

Either that, or we envision it as a place that's dark and cold, and where there's not a lot to do. Sort of like Duluth, Minn.

But death isn't at all like that.

Right now you're probably thinking, "Oh yeah? So, what exactly is death like, Mr. Transcendental Bigshot Wiseguy?"

I'll tell you.

A profound understanding of it came to me a few days ago while toiling in the great outdoors. Yard work, as the ancient Greeks knew, is conducive to philosophical insight.

In front of my homestead, the sweet gum, flowering crab apple and great big maple-type tree I've never managed to identify have been engaged in a race to drop their leaves before any other trees in the neighborhood. Their competitiveness has put me in the forefront of local leaf rakers, which means that my hand sores and muscle aches will have subsided by the time everyone else is being afflicted.

As anyone who has raked leaves seriously knows, the near-meditative repetition inherent in the task can induce a trance-like state. It was while in just such a condition of higher consciousness that I came to realize death is not falling asleep or even moving to a port city on Lake Superior.

No, death is the drying up of the last little bit of sticky resin that holds us onto the Great Tree of Existence, causing us to flush colorfully sick and swoon to the Lawn of Memory below.

We then sort of begin fermenting, emitting a wonderful but short-lived Perfume of Recollection, turn tan and crispy, and pile up on the Lawn, eventually indistinguishable from one another.

So many people have died since the dawn of humankind, it's impossible for the living to remember more than a minuscule fraction of them — those they loved in life, those who were famous, and so on. As the writer Milan Kundera says, history is but the slimmest thread of memory stretching across an ocean of what's been forgotten.

All right. So what happens next is a guy with a big nose and mustache comes along with the Giant Rake of Eternal Forgetfulness, and goes to work. Muttering darkly and raising a horrible, raw, red blister on the inside second joint of his thumb, he sweeps us deceased leaf people into ever-bigger piles that advance toward the Curb of Disremembrance, thus making room on the Lawn of Memory for those still green and cocky on the Tree above. Finally, he swooshes the piles out into the Endless Street of Oblivion.

What happens after that?

Beats me. All I know is they're out of my yard.

Hunter's Tale

Dave Babcock sighted the slide-action Remington 30.06 on the upper back of the large buck as it loped away 55 yards down the snow-covered trail. From beneath a canopy of snow-heavy evergreen boughs he aimed as close to the front shoulder as possible, hoping for a lung shot that would drop the animal instantly. A one-shot kill.

It was a little after 5 p.m. Saturday, Nov. 18, in a woods along the Sturgeon River in northern Otsego County, a few miles from Vanderbilt. The sky was darkening quickly. What little warmth the day had held was vanishing with the light; the temperature was 17 degrees.

Babcock fired. The buck's rear legs collapsed beneath it, but it remained standing on its forelegs. Babcock reloaded and took a step forward to finish it quickly, but the buck regained its feet, and when Babcock fired again, he missed. The buck climbed a small hill and disappeared into a thick wood of maples, poplars and pines.

In the failing light, Babcock followed. He found droplets of blood in the snow and markings that indicated a leg being dragged. The blood was not frothy, as though from the lungs. Babcock feared he had gut-shot the animal.

Suddenly the buck emerged from a stand of pines to the right and cantered across Babcock's path. The Remington was on safety; there was no time for a shot. Babcock pursued it into a cedar swamp beaver dams had created near the river.

It was dark now. The snow in the swamp was waist-high and the footing beneath it boggy and treacherous. New snow filled the air, erasing sky and treetops and all perspective.

Babcock was lost. His fervor to finish the chase and end the animal's suffering gave way to the realization he must escape this surreal and referenceless place.

He picked his way by flashlight through blackness, over the undulating snow and scrub. Unseen evergreen branches whacked him in the face with fistfuls of snow every few steps. Time seemed elongated, as slow as his progress. After an hour, he came upon a set of boot prints. He marked a tree and backtracked along the route he'd just come. When he came again to the marked tree, he knew the prints were his and it was safe to follow them out.

Babcock arrived at camp soaked, exhausted, overwrought. Detroit businessman Larry Shade, his hunting companion, had never seen him so shaken. Babcock talked feverishly of the buck all evening. He even suggested going back into the swamp that night to find it.

Shade talked him out of it. "That swamp is like hell," he said. "That's why the deer go there. Anyway, your deer is probably down, lying somewhere dead. First thing in the morning we'll go and find the carcass. Don't worry about it."

Babcock was 41, a Detroit police officer for more than 20 years, and a deer hunter since boyhood. He was not the sort for whom deer season was an excuse for gunplay or bar-hopping. He was the sort who could sit in a blind for hours watching the last leaf on a nearby limb struggle to keep its hold in a fluttering breeze. He savored the rusticity of camp life, the meditative solitude of the woods, the wariness of the prey.

He had pondered the contradictions of the hunt, and knew he could not resolve them. Killing a deer after a year's anticipation was matchlessly thrilling. Yet for him the kill was the worst moment of the hunt. Fellow feeling poured through the rifle's scope at the same instant lead flew from its barrel. The shot slew the quiet. The kill was a letdown; it meant the hunt was over.

Babcock spanned these contradictions with code: Try for the one-shot kill. Promptly end the suffering of a creature you wound. Eat the meat, save the hide, respect the life you took.

The two men went to bed at 10 o'clock. Babcock was usually an untroubled sleeper, but tonight he replayed his shot over and over in his mind. The thick gloves he'd been wearing because of the cold must have decreased his trigger- sensitivity. He must have failed to make sufficient allowance for the buck's rapid movement away from him as he fired.

Several times he climbed out of his sleeping bag to put an unnecessary log in the wood stove or to stand outside and look at the sky. Sometimes it was clear. Sometimes it snowed furiously and he would think of the buck's tracks being covered over. He stared toward the swamp and tried to envision the buck dead, but there was something in the dark that would not allow him to convince himself. The night became a long vigil.

Before sunup, Babcock left Shade on the trail and went into the swamp alone. The morning gave up its light so grudgingly it seemed a taunt to his eagerness. A little after 7, he came upon the tracks of four deer traveling in single file. The tracks approached the base of a partially uprooted tree. Two sets went to the left of it, one set to the right and one directly beneath it.

Babcock crawled under the tree and blew away the thin powdering of new snow from this set of tracks. Among them were pellets of frozen blood.

He followed the tracks for 30 feet and came upon a large indentation in the snow marked in several places by sizable clots of frozen blood. The buck had bedded here for a time. The wound must be to its haunch. The buck had pressed it against an area of packed snow to slow the bleeding and perhaps numb the pain, and when that area melted, it had squirmed to a new position so it could lay the wound against fresh snow.

Twenty yards beyond the first site was a second such indentation, and 10 feet from the river a third. In the third indentation was nearly a pint's worth of blood, frozen into a ball. Babcock picked it up and held it in his hand.

The tracks turned east along the water's edge and wound around a small cedar tree bent over with snow at the entrance to an especially congested part of the swamp. Babcock's eyes were cast down, tracking. Rising to look ahead, they fixed on the buck lying in the snow 65 feet ahead.

The buck got to its feet. Babcock expected it to bolt. It didn't. It turned its head slightly and locked its eyes on his. It seemed resigned:

Here I am.

It was too weak to flee. Babcock understood that. Yet he also understood that there had been a vigil last night down here, too. He got the feeling he and the buck, preoccupied with one another's existence, had passed the night in wakeful, inarticulate communication. He wondered if its nocturnal risings — three indentations — had coincided with his own, if its physical squirmings had paralleled his mental discomforts.

Those eyes fixed on yours, they could turn you against deer hunting forever.

Or they could confirm you in its mystical appeal.

Babcock had forgotten he was carrying a rifle.

He raised the Remington abruptly, half-expecting the animal, even now, to bound away. Sighting just below the little white patch on the buck's throat, he squeezed into existence the worst moment of the hunt.

Rest of the Story

In case you've been pondering the fate of T. Grinch,
Arrested last year in the Christmas-theft pinch,
The latest news is, after 12 months in stir,
His release on parole is about to occur.

The news of his crime took up this entire page,
And prompted outpourings of sorrow and rage.
At length, Grinch repented and gave back the loot,
Forswearing forever his Santy Claus suit.

His trial held Who-ville in televised thrall,
As Max, his poor dog, took the stand and told all.
Max sang in exchange for a sentence decrease —
A new lease on life for a new life on leash.

A credible witness, the jury decided,
Not evil, but merely by Grinchy misguided,
To dress like a reindeer and power the sleigh
That Grinch used to haul Who-ville's Christmas away.

Poor Grinch wept so loud he was heard through the town:
"My heart's grown three sizes since all that went down!
"I'm certain, in my case, probation's deserved."

The judge gave him two years (including time served).

In prison, Grinch proved to be no callow dope
(He never bent over to pick up the soap).
He worked hard in voc-ed and learned to cut hair.
He got quite adept at small-motor repair.

Lest his oversized heart get him into a jam,
He swore off roast beast and all green eggs and ham.
He worked out with weights, every barbell and winch,
And molded himself into quite a he-Grinch.

But not just his corpus has Grinchy attended,
He's also his spiritual outlook amended.
No longer a grumpy old cave-dwelling wraith,
He's fully embraced the Baha'i life and faith.

He's sworn to love everyone, Whats, Whys and Whos,
And accept them for being however they choose.
No wonder the gov'nor (while cutting the arts)
Felt cutting his sentence showed mercy and smarts.

The Who-ville parole board must now decide whether
Grinch will be freed on electronic tether,
Or placed in a halfway house geared for the meek,
And call his parole worker two times a week.

Response up in Who-ville's been, overall, good,
Though some fear the prospect of him in their 'hood.
Still undetermined — a real chitchat stopper —
Is, should there be banishment from Who-ville proper?

Job prospects in town are now smaller than ants,
With layoffs at all Who-ville's stressed zike-bike plants.
It's hard for a Boy Scout to find much employ,
Much less an ex-con with a rep as killjoy.

"I'll earn my way back into Who-ville's good graces,"
Swears Grinch. "I'm prepared to kick out all the traces.
"The market is awful, but, see, I'm not nervous.
"I'll just give myself to community service.

"I'll volunteer carving roast beast that is boneless,
"And serving it up to Who-villian homeless.
"I'll firmly resist all recidivist yen.
"They'll never get me in the Big House again."

Ice Fishing Has Its Snags

If I'm ever to transform myself into a true Michigan man, sooner or later I had to face up to one of the most daunting tests of all: ice fishing.

Now, I've heard all the sniggering about ice fishing; for a long time, whenever the subject came up, I employed the line, "So, what do you do with all that ice after you catch it?"

Yet there's something vaguely philosophical about hooded figures on a silent, frozen plain staring down through holes into an alien world.

And vague philosophy, well, you might say it is my life.

So after a band of native Michigan men made it impossible for me to decline, I recently found myself in the frigid calm of the state's northland, glad to be away from office buildings, parking problems and all the other things that crowd people who don't ice fish.

My companions were members of our regular basketball group. They hunt deer and troll for lake trout and know how to get boats back onto trailers. They own beards, flannel shirts, down vests. They foul like Cossacks. I've got a long way to go to catch up to them.

We rendezvoused up north in a small-town saloon where two tough-looking women shot eight-ball, and a man without a nose watched us from the bar. Soon we were a couple of miles out on Higgins Lake, separated from 42 feet of water by 16 inches of ice.

It was beautiful in an otherworldly kind of way: blue dome of sunshot sky, heat and cold alternating on the face with every turn of the head, Christmas trees stuck in the ice to mark old pike-spearing holes. I took in all this beauty for 20 minutes before repairing to the coop one of our number had built.

Thanks to a small wood stove, the temperature inside pushed 70. We jigged for perch through four holes in the floor, sipped beer, steamed hot dogs on the stove, caught nothing, until the sun dropped and the wood ran out.

We spent the night at a spacious, one-room deer camp lent by a group of local outdoorsmen who treated us to a feed of braised squirrel. After a few hands of seven-and-a-half, I was ready for a top bunk.

I'd envisioned falling asleep surrounded by a night stunned to holy quiet by the bitter northland cold. Maybe hearing an owl call (if those critters do that sort of thing on those kinds of nights) as I went under. But a wall-mounted stereo speaker a few feet from my head throbbed with Clarence (Frogman) Henry, and the most durable of our contingent played cards and nipped and talked till past three. Near five, someone finally turned out the bright overhead lights.

It was 11 below when I got up after 2½ hours' sleep. This time, I borrowed every piece of clothing the others would part with, and could barely maneuver to drive my car to the shore.

This day, some fish would die at the hands of our group. But not, specifically, at mine. The perch avoided my bait like it was selling insurance.

But you don't have to catch fish to pass the ice-fishing test. You only have to achieve understanding.

Later, on shore for the drive home, I peeled eight layers of clothing and thanked my friends. I took a deep draught of the crackling air and a last look at the profound emptiness, knowing I understood, and went to my car.

There was a parking ticket on the windshield.

Stout Hearts Hit the Streets

Give us more winter storms like we had last week.

In a certain hardy breed of us North-dwellers, large dumpings of snow and inch-thick encrustations of ice rouse a spirit of ableness fast asleep when roads are dry and business is as usual.

If you fit the category and happened to be out driving, as I was, in the teeth of the storm Wednesday night, you know what I mean.

A surreal, feathery loveliness lit by sodium vapor lights filled the air and rounded the landscape. The expressway, piling with snow, lost its lanes. Some drivers pulled off and took refuge beneath bridges, their emergency lights blinking timidity.

But not us, baby. We pressed on, trailblazing when necessary. We kept a moderate, continuous speed, avoiding sudden turns or brakings, our hand steady on the wheel, our gaze steely as we steered into occasional skids. Just like our fathers taught us all those years ago.

We awoke earlier than usual the next day, and with no small amount of eagerness. We looked out the window and, just as we'd thought, the cold sky was still discharging onto the ground.

Now came the real test — getting to work through the morass the storm had spent the entire night preparing for us. With each school closing announced by J.P. over the radio, our resolve hardened. People all over the place would be giving themselves permission to pass up the challenge. Not us. Baby.

We eschewed the expressways, of course. They'd be clogged with poor, baa-ing sheep stuck in long parking formations, anxious and uncomprehending, unable to escape. No, we took to the surface streets, where there were more detour options, and we could more easily skirt stranded motorists who'd lost their nerve.

Frozen rain materialized on our heated windshields, then died in smears beneath the wipers. Roostertails of snow-slush-ice, heavy as mud, rose from the wheels of adjacent cars and destroyed visibility for breathless instants.

It took a while, but we made it.

Strode into work, on time, a bit early, even, with snowy boots and a self-pleased smile. Gradually, a band of similarly stouthearted colleagues formed around us. We speculated about absent coworkers. Stuck on freeways. Still at home, peering nervously from their windows. Poor babes.

So they weren't here. No problem. We who'd made it would pitch in, do our work and the work of the missing, too. We didn't resent it a bit, either. We were as aglow with comradeship as the expressway was with sodium vapor the night before.

Hey, it occurred to us, who are these people who whine about winter and pine to live in the humidity and decay of Florida? This is MICHIGAN. You want cold, clear lakes and trout streams in summer, you got to have this now.

Balmier climes give the average person no equivalent opportunity to test his or her mettle. Oh, Florida has its hurricanes and California its earthquakes, but those are phenomena people can only flee or hide from.

Winter storms, well, they challenge your determination to function, to summon your pluck and by sheer force of will hold up the great edifice of human productive routine.

Around here, that's the way we earn spring.

LOOK AT IT THIS WAY

CHAPTER THREE

An Act of Faith

She had never done this before, she said, tamping the emotion in her throat, and was finding it "pitiful, degrading. I'm on the verge of tears talking to you."

She was a pale, freckled woman in a beige jacket and light blue jeans torn at one knee. Her hair was tugged back in a ponytail and showed gray at the base of her neck. Her mouth was thin and gave a faint, false impression of toothlessness.

An infant in a red crocheted cap murmured in the baby harness at her chest. A toddler, a restless, inquisitive boy, was tethered to her wrist by a length of blue-and-white cloth.

She stood at the entrance to the parking lot across Canfield from the Traffic Jam restaurant last Thursday evening, and her first words to me, spoken softly, were: "Excuse me, sir, do you have some spare change?"

I had been panhandled countless times in Detroit, but never by a mother and her children. She was rational and sober; she and her children looked clean and nourished, although there was about them the vague mustiness of need.

I handed over two quarters and drove away, pursued by the thought of her. After a few blocks, I went back and asked her if she would talk.

She said she was 36, her daughter 8 months, her son 3. She told me her name, but asked that I not use it.

"I'm newly divorced," she said. "I am for the first time in my life totally alone. I have never been on Social Services before, but I am now. And my check is four days late. That's why I'm out here. I have no diapers and I also have no milk. I'm only trying to get $4.50. This is the first time in my life I have ever asked anybody for a dime.

"And it kind of upsets me (her voice faltered) ... because, you know, when somebody honestly, sincerely needs something, I have gone out of my way to do something for such unfortunate people. But now that I am in a very bad predicament ... I have never ..."

For a moment, she couldn't go on.

"This is so degrading to me because I'm not a dumb person. I have an excellent work background behind me and a good educational background. I'm not desperate enough to go out and sell myself, or anything like that. I've gotten about $1.50. I need $4.50, and when I get it I'm going home. And pray that my check will be there tomorrow." I gave her $10. She seemed moved. We parted.

I had an impulse to follow her, to see if she went for her diapers and milk, but I quickly realized I had no right.

Ten dollars is not much; I could have given her more. The difference between what I gave and what I could have are the wages of the skepticism abiding in everything that has to do with money.

For many years, I refused to give to panhandlers. But a friend of mine, a student of philosophy, convinced me that amounted to making all manner of potentially unfair judgments about complete strangers. It took me a long time to accustom myself to swallowing the anger, revulsion and edgy disinclination to be duped, but now I usually part with my pocket change when asked.

Whether a person begs from unlucky circumstances or manipulative instincts or a lack of shame ultimately doesn't matter. The issue is not their worth, but my willingness to make a tiny, specific act of faith in a very generalized version of humanity. A version whose war wounds are real, whose job really was just lost, whose bumming of dimes really is aimed at a bowl of chili. Or whose late welfare check really has created a desperation for diapers and milk.

Untie the Ribbons

No, I haven't put out my American flag. Neither have I tied yellow ribbons on the trees in the yard.

This does not mean I've been indifferent to the fate of the American soldiers in the Persian Gulf. Far from it. Grant me one wish today, and I would ask that all the dead of this war be restored to their suffering families and the rest returned home without so much as mussed hair.

But the flags and the yellow ribbons bring me down.

In my mind they've become something other than benign symbols of country and of hope for happy reunion. They've come to signify enthusiasm for war, and for an American future that is bleak and troubling to contemplate.

I sometimes wonder also if their purpose hasn't been to cow into silence those who've opposed the war. Who is their target? Saddam Hussein, who cannot see them, or me?

Most people have flown them primarily because they've felt the need to demonstrate support for the troops. They've wanted to obliterate the uncomfortable memory, much harped on by some Vietnam combat veterans, of soldiers returning unloved from an unpopular war a generation ago. People long for the unanimity of sentiment that characterized the home front of World War II, our last "good" war, from which we emerged dominant instead of dispirited.

The problem is, in the complicated present all this flagging and ribboning has been a little too easy.

At bottom, the Gulf War has not been about good vs. evil (we've often supported brutal tyrants, including the now demonized Saddam Hussein). It has not been about the sanctity of United Nations resolutions (we've ignored every one that relates to Palestinian rights). It has not been, fundamentally, even about oil (although I wonder if our government would be so hot to liberate Kuwait if that emirate produced only figs).

What this war has really been about is the role the United States will play in the world from now on. Apparently, we are going to be a force primarily through our high-tech, astonishingly expensive and newly public-relations-proficient military, now cleansed of the "stain" of Vietnam. We are to be the one country that can get its way anywhere in the world through armed might.

But this is not 1945. We've defeated not a major world evil but a crude local cutthroat. Moreover, we do not finish this war in possession of 50 percent of the world's industrial productive capacity, as we did then.

The world's ascendant powers, Japan and the Europe that will unite economically next year, know that the great weapons of modern international competition are peaceful — efficient industries and aggressive trade. These weapons are forged by superior systems of education, public health and infrastructure at home. Military power is less and less relevant.

The Gulf War and the facile patriotic feeling it has engendered obscure that we are way behind in our thinking. That our national priorities should be not smart bombs but smart kids, not lower rates of "collateral damage" but lower rates of infant mortality and drug abuse.

These are complicated, urgent matters on which the security of our way of life truly depends. You cannot address them by tying a yellow ribbon on a lamppost. You cannot resolve them by setting a flag out to snap in the breeze.

Melville at the Helms

Knock, knock.

"Yes?"

"You Melville? H. Melville?"

"That's right. The 'H' is for 'Herman.' "

"Yeah, well, lookahere, Herman, my name's Dowd. With the National Endowment for the Arts? Formerly with Sen. Helms' office? I come to talk to you about this here book you hope to get a grant for."

"I must say, I'm a bit surprised to receive a personal visitation."

"We only visit what you call your borderline cases. And that's what you are, Herman. A borderline case. I wanna talk to you about this book to see if we can clear up the concerns NEA's got."

"Well, of course. Do come in."

"Good. Now, let's get down to cases. First off, this hero of yours. This Ishmael. That a Jew name?"

"Well, it's certainly Old Testament, although Ishmael is Presbyterian."

"That was a real good answer, Herman. Let me write that down. A lotta good Christian taxpayers might not be real happy supporting a book they think's all about somebody who don't believe in Jesus. On the other hand, lots of folks do love the first part of the Bible. OK, what about this guy named Queequeg? He some kinda nigra?"

"Actually, if you peruse with diligence you'll find he's a Pacific islander."

"Oh, yeah. Here it is. From 'Kokovoko.' Dang queer name."

"Well, of course it doesn't exist in reality. I refer to it as an 'uncharted is-land.' You see, my desire is to portray a whaling crew that represents all the peoples of the world, and ..."

"I don't know, Herman. We're getting a lot of flak these days over all the kids in this country who don't know nothing about geography. And here you go makin' up places, and wanting taxpayers to help pay for it. Couldn't we just say he's from Atlanta or Phoenix?"

"Now, just a moment, my good man. What do you mean, 'we'?"

"Don't get touchy. Let's just mark this item for further discussion."

" ... this is not *ours*, but rather what I consider to be *my* masterp- ..."

"I said, Herman. Let's move *on*. Take a look at this part where Ishmael and Queequeg go beddy-bye together in the Spouter Inn. Now, is that really necessary?"

"It's symbolic. It is a precursor of the common fate they will encounter upon Capt. Ahab's whaling ship, and by extension the common fate of all human beings on ..."

"But, Herman, they are sleeping together. In the same bed. Two *fellers!* Not only that, but one of 'em's a 'harpooner.' Now I know you artistes are real proud of your sly little images and all, but don't you think that's a lit-tle obvious in its homersexual overtones?"

"Just what, Mr. Dowd, would you alternatively suggest?"

"They could just shoot a game of eight ball, like regular buddies. They could go bowling. Pick up a coupla gals."

"Good Lord."

"We're a little troubled also by the whales. Bad enough the animal rights nutballs are gonna be all over us, but do these whales have to be sperm whales? That's awful reproductive sounding. Makes a lot of us real uncomfortable. Especially that scene where the crew's sittin' around han-dlin' the damn stuff, breaking up the lumps and whatnot. You got your blue whales, you got your gray whales, you got your killer whales — why not hunt those critters instead? I mean, whales is whales, as far as the aver-age taxpayer is concerned. Now, about the title."

"I thought you'd get 'round to that."

"I got no problem with the 'Moby,' of course. No one'll know what the hell that means anyway. But as for the other word ... well. Herman, inno-cent little children are going to see this book on the shelves."

"Perhaps then I ought to rename it to evoke the utmost benign associa-tion in children. Would the NEA find 'Moby Breast' more to its liking?"

"Aw, *heck,* no. That's worse. I was thinkin' more of a title that'd reassure people from the git-go. Something like, 'Angling with Ahab.' Or, how about this: 'You Can Call Me Ishmael, But That Don't Mean I'm a Jew.' That one's got a real nice artistic ring to it, don't you think?"

One Strike and He's Out

Over the years, my teenage daughters have seen their old man equivocate and change his mind many times in his quest to bring them safely to useful adulthood.

On one point, however, he has been adamant.

Neither of them is to have anything further to do with any male who has even hinted at laying hands on her in anger.

This rule is to apply no matter how much she loves him. It is to apply no matter how many children she has had by him, or how economically dependent she is on him. One blow or intimation of it instantly changes the landscape. The relationship is finished. There are to be no second chances, no opportunities for a pattern to evolve.

In short, my daughters are not to wait around to see if the male in question turns out to be a David James.

Earlier this week, James transformed his family's Taylor home into a slaughterhouse. He murdered his wife, Robin, and their toddler and their infant, then erased his own existence. There was hardly a lack of warning. Neighbors said they'd previously seen James strike his wife with a telephone, throw her to the ground in the backyard, chase her down the street with a baseball bat.

Let's be clear. David James was the criminal, and the guilt is entirely on his head.

Yet, in the sorrow and anger that welled up in this father of daughters when he read of the tragedy, one question refused to be dismissed:

Why in the hell was Robin James still in that house?

I know that battered women frequently feel trapped. They stay with their tormentors because they have nowhere else to go, or cannot afford to leave, or fear their children will suffer from the family separation. Still, if they knew for certain Robin James' fate was to be their own, they'd almost certainly find a way to leave. Underlying it all, I think, is the delusion that somehow their men will change and become gentled.

There is another side, too, I realize. I don't know specifically about David James' case, but men who beat women are commonly the products of families in which violence was as ordinary a part of domestic life as Thursday meat loaf. (All the more reason for women to remove their children from such men — so that the young ones won't carry on the family tradition when they grow up.)

The ultimate solution to domestic violence is less violent men. Good luck. That will require a major cultural shift. We will have to do something about the easy association of fistedness with manliness, especially in the minds of boys. We will have to end the commercial sexual exploitation of women, which amounts to treating them like objects. If you can objectify a woman for sex, you can objectify her for anything else, including a pounding.

For women caught in the fear and dispiritedness of physically abusive relationships, there is not a lot to be easily done.

The next generation of women, however, can be given a head start. Today's girls can be taught, fervently, that they are not helpless before the specter of Robin James' fate. That they need only be suitably ruthless suitably early. That the unshakable principle is, the first time he so much as grabs your wrist in anger, he disqualifies himself from your life.

Home Field Disadvantage

One night last week while the clear sky over Tiger Stadium went from blue to turquoise to navy, and the homeboys pounded hell out of Seattle, it finally dawned on me:

This place is history. Practically gone already.

I'd been resisting the thought for a long time, preferring to believe that those fighting to save Tiger Stadium would win out simply because their cause is right. My little epiphany came while sitting with friends in second-tier box seats along the first base line. We seemed almost to hover over the left shoulder of Detroit's Cecil Fielder; seemed almost close enough to flick a popcorn kernel down and ping the big first baseman on the hat, if we'd wanted to. We hear he's a pretty good-natured fellow. Maybe he'd look up and we'd give him a clench-fisted "all right, Cess," and he'd grin.

The field, as always, was a galloping carpet of jade below. We could see well all that transpired on it, practically from foul line to foul line, without moving our heads. No other major league ballpark I've been in delivers such expanse with such intimacy, and thus makes a spectator feel such a part of the proceedings.

This was exactly what was wrong, I realized.

In modern, mass-market America, the average consumer doesn't get this close to anything this good. Not for 10 bucks.

No matter what sort of new park eventually results from all the posturing by the Tigers organization, Wayne County and the City of Detroit, the intimacy will be lost. Ticket-buyers will sit at respectful distances from the Brahmin in uniform.

The people trying to save the old stadium have got a couple of things wrong.

They've convinced themselves the sports-buying public is on their side. They see that public as loyal, aware of history, good at heart. But, really, they are talking only about themselves. The great mass of the sports-buying public is cynical, entertainment-addicted and readily manipulated.

The stadium-savers, being lovers, are blind — blind to the fact that in the modern professional sports industry the game is secondary to the entertainment experience. People will be easily induced to patronize a glittering new stadium, electronicized to the nines, no matter how deficient the place is in soul. Just so long as the sound system can really crank it out, man.

Those the lovers oppose see this very clearly. They are men of commerce who cannot afford the myopia of sentiment. That Cobb once slid on this very spot; that Greenberg once reached that pole in the upper deck — well, put a dollar value on it; tell us how it's convertible toward Alan Trammell's salary this year.

Pity the lovers. Their love is doomed to dissolve in bitterness. For Tom Monaghan will have his new entertainment palace, the crowds will come, and the lovers will be left with nothing but the ache of loss, the fury of impotence.

Personally, I feel a little like someone who's come to accept that a loved one soon will die. The best thing to do is get the grieving over with now, in advance, and make the most of the star-spattered nights still left to the old place.

Realities on Parade

Let's have another parade.

Come on, what do you say? A parade even bigger and more colorful than the great big Desert Storm parade in New York. Even more honest-to-God, up-to-date American than the one in Washington last weekend.

Bet we can do it for less than $12 million, too.

We don't want to hold this particular parade in Washington, though. Washington is a fantasyland where well-heeled people can make things seem what they're not. New York would be OK, but it's still cleaning up. So let's hold this one in Newark or Detroit or some other place where the real drama of national life is being played out.

It won't be easy deciding who should lead this parade, but I think kids. Everybody likes kids.

How about we start with a contingent from the neonatal wards of the public hospitals? A little fresh air might be good for those twitchy little crack babies. And what do you say to a couple of empty cribs on wheels to symbolize the high number of Americans who don't make it to age 1?

We could follow this with a marching band of kids from the poorest elementary schools, silently playing patriotic tunes on make-believe instruments. They'd honor the fact that 2.2 million more kids live in poverty now than did 10 years ago.

And right on their heels a delegation of headphone-wearing, subliterate teens ready for release into the work force. They'd carry banners declaring, "The Futre of Our Nashun," and "Mr. Emploir, Here We Cum."

These will be followed by several large cages containing live prison inmates. Homage to the national incarceration rate, the world's highest.

The most exotic contingent of all will come next: the de-institutionalized, untreated mentally ill from large cities across the land. They will wear hooded parkas in the hot summer sun and carry plastic grocery bags straining with inexplicable objects. In and out of formation they will wander, jabbering and imploring, weeping and bellowing.

That high-energy display will call for a respite. So the next unit will be families not covered by health insurance. Nice, slow-moving people these, fearful of falling and being hurt, dreading illness.

Then, hooray, the clowns — a contingent of addicts. All ages. All social classes. Disoriented alcoholics with flowering nose capillaries. Rank, shuffling crackheads. Nodding heroin junkies. Wobbly-legged pill-poppers. Agitated coke zombies.

On and on the great parade will come:

Big-city mayors with pants pockets turned inside out. Middle-income people bent over with tuition debt. Somber women of reproductive age with chains draped over their abdomens. Laid-off factory hands chanting the names of underdeveloped countries where their jobs have been exported. Delegations of the working poor in fast-food restaurant uniforms, trying to look grateful for their futureless, minimum-wage jobs.

Just as the big parade in Washington featured glittering weaponry, this one will feature infrastructure: rusted girders from highway bridges, giant potholes excavated from state roads, worn-out airliners with loosening rivets.

One heck of a parade we could have.

But how many patriotic Americans would have the stomach to come watch?

Come as You Are

Two cheers for the Detroit Board of Education's efforts to establish standards of dress for students in the city's public high schools.

Banning students from wearing gold chains and Triple F.A.T. Goose down jackets and sneakers that cost $100 might prevent another kid from being shot by someone trying to steal his clothes, as happened to two Detroit students recently. No one will be able to prove if it does, of course, but it might. One cheer.

It's nice also to see civil authorities making a statement against the mindless, price-tag materialism to which teenagers, with their incomplete perspectives, are especially vulnerable. Another cheer.

Beyond that, however, I don't much like people messing with the way other people dress. In the hierarchy of man-made tyrannies, dress codes are right up there with high fashion and religious orthodoxy.

My older daughter went to a grade school with a very strict dress code. By the time she was in eighth grade, she was practically bursting with impatience at the stultifying rules.

She's since gone on to a high school that doesn't restrict the way kids dress except within obvious reason. It's been kind of fun watching her survey the styles of the different tribes at her school (preppies, punks, jocks, etc.) and experiment with unusual combinations of items.

True, the first time she set off to school in an old, baggy sweater and thermal long underwear beneath a pair of huge boxer shorts, I had to remind myself why I was being so tolerant. And it took a few wearings to get used to men's pajama bottoms being rolled and draped at the hems and worn as trousers.

By now she has tuned in a style of dressing that embraces everything from handsome blouses to oddball hats to my old Army fatigues.

What I like best is that her raiment seems to reflect an evolving notion of herself as someone unique, creative, informal, a little noir, a little offbeat, fun. I think she looks great, and to heck with what other adults may think of her clothes. They can go chafe in their neckties and panty hose.

For most of my adult life I have myself resisted dressing according to sober convention. I'm seldom to be found in the office in anything more formal than wrinkled cotton slacks and a sweater. Comfort should rule, I believe, and no more autocratically than in the workplace.

My daughter's sense of style has accelerated this tendency. One of the advantages of having teenage daughters is that, through the gifts they give, they nudge you into sartorial waters you'd otherwise not have risked.

The Christmas before last, my daughters bought me a pair of Girbaud corduroy pants so wide you could smuggle a couple of Frenchmen into the country in each leg. At first I wore them only around the house when I was feeling whimsical. Now I'm in them more than any others I own.

They are the warmest, loosest, softest, most billowy, comforting pants I've ever worn, and who cares if an occasional old lady at the supermarket snickers. They make a person feel at peace and thoroughly human, a friend to all and a threat to none.

If I had the authority, I'd make them mandatory for everyone.

Defensive Drive-thru

Good afternoon, Mr. Jederman, and welcome to your Super Sobriety Check Lane.

On your way back to the office from lunch, are you? Don't worry, this won't take long at all. Especially if you give us a little cooperation.

We just want to have a look at you to make sure you're in compliance with the laws against drunk driving. Want to see if your eyes seem normal, want to sniff the air around your face, want to check for any open bottles that might be lying on the seat. That sort of thing.

If you haven't done anything wrong, you have nothing to worry about. You might not even have to blow into the breathalyzer. See, it's not you we're after. It's them, the drunk drivers. We all know how dangerous drunk drivers are.

Of course, while we've got you here, we might as well kill a couple of birds with one stone, so to speak.

Some people who don't drink have been known to smoke a little pot or sniff up an occasional line of the white stuff. We don't have to tell you that drivers high on those substances are a real menace.

So, we'd better have a look at the old urine, too, Mr. J., just to confirm to everyone and anyone that you're the law-abiding citizen and trustworthy motorist we're pretty confident you are. There's a portable john and laboratory in that small van over there. Our lab techs will have the results lickety-split. After all, they process thousands of specimens every day.

Let us reiterate. We're not after you. We're after the guilty ones, the ones who make all of our lives riskier.

Here's something we bet you're not aware of: Drivers who fall asleep behind the wheel are a major cause of fatal auto accidents.

This one, unfortunately, is a little tougher to check for. Sorry about that.

The only way we can distinguish you — and by extension protect you — from such people is to have you take a Multiple Sleep Latency Test. Here's how it works:

You go into that blue bus there, we hook you up to an EEG and have you lie down on a comfortable bed in a specially designed compartment that's dark and quiet. Then we time how long it takes you to doze off. The shorter the time, the more of a hazard you are to the other people who share the road with you. Very simple.

Did we say, "you"? Well, we don't really mean you. You look like a perfectly chipper, well-rested, responsible citizen who can be trusted to keep his glimmers wide open while behind the wheel. At least for right now.

And that should just about do it.

Except for the Hostility and Direction of Hostility Examination.

We've got some new studies indicating that tense, hostile drivers are an important factor in highway death rates. One of our psychologists will explain the exam and fit you with the electrode cap in a minute.

You might not believe this, but some people — pretty darned suspicious ones, if you ask us — have a problem with answering questions about their sexual fantasies and relationships with their mothers and the geometrical shapes they hate most. They make us extra appreciative of people like you, people who have nothing to hide.

So, good luck with the tests, although we seriously doubt an upstanding citizen like yourself really needs luck.

And have a very, very safe day.

Out on Luck

Before Ollie North gets subsumed in a false heroism by the famously forgetful American people, permit me to do my part to derail this train in the station.

The other day, U.S. District Judge Gerhard Gesell dropped all charges against Ollie, the sanctimonious pin-up boy of the nutbar right. Ollie immediately declared he'd been "fully, completely vindicated" and "totally exonerated, fully, completely."

Funny. I was under the impression the judge threw out North's convictions because his 1989 trial might have been affected by testimony North gave under immunity to Congress in 1987.

Ollie, in other words, got off on a technicality. He beat the rap on a legalistic fine point.

Full, complete vindication? Total, full, complete exoneration? I don't think so. A crook who lucked out, is more like it.

Ollie had admitted — practically boasted — that he secretly sold American arms to our good friend Iran, and used the proceeds to supply weapons to the Nicaraguan contras, then lied to Congress about it.

This last was in utter contempt of democratically enacted American law. But Ollie was acting in accordance with the higher law of blind zealotry.

When the evidence was weighed in light of the lower law the rest of us must abide by, Ollie came up guilty on three felony counts: destroying official documents, accepting an illegal gratuity and aiding in the obstruction of Congress.

Talk about your squeaky clean patriot.

This week, however, Ollie "walked," and for exactly the same reason many a street thug has: His constitutional entitlement to a fair trial, guaranteed by that lower law for which he has such contempt, was violated.

Ordinarily, the wild-eyed right goes ballistic whenever this happens. In Ollie's case, they're so jubilant they're probably planning a few celebratory schoolbook burnings.

Ollie is free now to devote himself full time to advancing the agenda of the Freedom Alliance, collecting 25,000 bucks a speech in the process.

He may now without official blemish plump for: The defeat of the left-wing Congress (what a joke; it's hard enough to find a real Democrat in Congress these days, much less a bona fide leftster). The muzzling of the (political Neanderthals will want to sneer here) "liberal" press. The re-establishment of the "traditional" values of the "traditional" family (you know, Dad working, Mom at home with the kids). The roughly two-thirds of American families too socially and economically stressed to adopt that model can presumedly just go to hell.

Yeah, the O-man is officially back on the streets again, all right, and maybe even headed for elective office.

Those of us who believe in freedom of expression, the rule of law and the right to live our private lives any way we please had best be watching our backs.

Set Ahmad Free

The time has come for Gov. James Blanchard to set Ahmad Abdur-Rahman free.

There are cases in which justice transcends the ordinary application of the law, and Abdur-Rahman's is one of them.

Abdur-Rahman is serving a life sentence without parole for first-degree murder. That conjures images of rapist-killers, contract killers, cold-blooded takers of human life for personal gain or gratification, remorseless miscreants beyond any corrective touch.

None of these apply to Abdur-Rahman.

He has never killed anyone.

His sentence was the result of a critical error in judgment on his part when he was 19, of a climate of racial fear and retribution that existed at the time, and of a law that has since been recognized as unfair and reinterpreted by the state judiciary.

Now Abdur-Rahman, formerly known as Ronald Irwin, has spent his entire adulthood — 18 of his 38 years — in prison. He is considered a model inmate. "At this point in time, we would parole him, except for the life sentence," says William Hudson, chairman of the state parole board.

Abdur-Rahman's only hope is having his sentence commuted to make him eligible for parole. Only the governor can give commutations.

During two terms of office, Blanchard has commuted the sentence of but one prisoner, in 1985. In his State of the State message this year, he said he does not intend to release any of the 1,300 prisoners serving life-without-parole sentences, many of whom were convicted not of murder, but of being major drug dealers.

There is irony in this. Abdur-Rahman is in prison, not for dealing drugs, but for engaging in vigilantism against them.

Tom Scott, Blanchard's press spokesman, says the governor doesn't know of Abdur-Rahman or his case.

I hope he will read this, and see his way clear to a second commutation.

Abdur-Rahman and three other young members of the Black Panther Party raided an old mansion on Virginia Park Avenue in Detroit early on Easter Sunday 1971. Party leaders, some of whom likely were police informants, had led them to believe the place was a heroin den.

The party considered heroin dealers parasites on the black community. Some of its members, among them Abdur-Rahman, organized into armed squads and invaded dope houses, flushing drugs down toilets and expropriating dealers' money for such community projects as the free breakfast program the Black Panthers ran for poor children.

The raids were exceedingly dangerous, and the raiders kept none of the money for themselves. Abdur-Rahman, who held a romantic view of himself as a revolutionist fighting for his people, lived in poverty.

The house on Virginia Park was no dope house, but the communal residence of 15 Wayne State University students and other young people. One of the Panthers held a rifle on the assembled occupants while Abdur-Rahman and the others searched the house for money and drugs.

While they searched, a young man named Franklin Abramson, who was among those being guarded, moved to quiet his barking dog. The man with the rifle shoved him with the gun, which discharged, killing Abramson.

Abdur-Rahman was on another floor of the house when the gun went off.

Thanks to a police informant, the four raiders were arrested within a few days and charged with first-degree murder. All were given the opportunity to plead guilty to lesser charges. Only Abdur-Rahman refused, foolishly.

At that time, the law allowed a person to be found guilty of first-degree murder if he was involved in committing another felony (in this case, armed robbery) during which a person died. The law now requires that a defendant have intended to kill someone.

Abdur-Rahman's entire prior criminal record consisted of one misdemeanor, also incurred in connection with his activities as a Black Panther. But given the old law and the animosity society at large held for the strutting, belligerent Panthers, his conviction and sentencing to life without parole were nearly a foregone conclusion.

Abdur-Rahman's accomplices long since have been paroled; he has already been incarcerated six years longer than any of the others.

The man who killed Franklin Abramson has been free since 1983.

Abdur-Rahman sits in a visitors' room at G. Robert Cotton Correctional Facility in Jackson, clad in crisp plaid shirt and precisely creased blue jeans. He is a trim, ascetic man who eschews smoking, alcohol and drugs. He does yoga, and meditates every day.

For 11 years, he has been a devout orthodox Muslim, rising by 5:30 a.m. to pray for the first of five times daily, and living by rigorous Koranic standards of hygiene and morality. Islam, he says, has given him the strength and stability that have enabled him to bear his long imprisonment.

While in prison, he has earned a bachelor's degree in sociology from Wayne State, compiling a near-straight-A average, and credits toward a master's degree in Near Eastern studies from the University of Michigan. He has earned certificates as a paralegal and in video production, marketable skills both.

He passes his days reading, especially in comparative religions and philosophy, counseling younger prisoners, and dealing with not always sympathetic prison authorities on behalf of the 20 other active Muslim inmates who elected him imam, or leader. He is currently a litigant in a religious discrimination suit against prison authorities.

The Black Panthers' anti-drug crusade, however reckless its execution, seems to him almost vindicated in light of what drug addiction has wrought in black society since. "It's been said the drug plague in America has been to black men a holocaust," he says. "If a person knew that, wouldn't he have been justified in doing anything he could to prevent it? At the time, we in the Panther party saw this holocaust building. We saw what heroin was beginning to do. We thought we were justified in going to extreme measures in stopping it."

For nearly two decades, he has watched the stream of young black men — increasingly ill educated, lacking moral direction, caught up in the sale and use of drugs — flow into the state prison system. In his mind's eye, he sees himself on the other side of the prison wall helping stanch the flow.

"In the black subculture," he says, "crime and drugs are not just an issue of economics, they're an issue of power. Of powerless men finding ways to feel power. A drug dealer has the two main things everybody wants: He's got money and he's got dope. People who won't do what he wants for dope will do it for money. I believe I have developed some ways to teach young persons early how to have a sense of their own inner power, without having to use these exploitive means."

Dr. Gloria House, an associate professor of humanities at Wayne State, has known Abdur-Rahman since 1974, when she taught in a Wayne State program at Jackson prison. She has been leading a community effort in Detroit to have his case brought to the attention of the governor. Among those who have interceded are Elliott Hall, Ford Motor Co. vice president for Washington affairs, Edward Vaughn, executive assistant to the mayor of Detroit, and state Rep. Carolyn Kilpatrick, D-Detroit.

"Having had to discipline himself, Ahmad knows how to help other young people achieve that level of discipline," House says. "He's taught English, Arabic, literature, Islam. He's been a big brother to younger guys who have come in. Although he's in prison, he is a counselor to many of the people on the outside who have been in touch with him. He has deepened his humanity so much.

"We don't have to wait until he's out to see what kind of person he'd be. We've seen what he's become under the worst of conditions. They've made it difficult for him because he stands up for what is right, not just for himself, but for other men. When he's out and able to make his own life and create his own home, it's going to be so much easier for him to be this extraordinary human being he's become."

Abdur-Rahman longs to be included on the extensive list of young black radicals who have matured into educators, social workers, community leaders. "What I would be involved in were I free," he says, "would be seen as proving that my release was, as far as dealing with prisoners, one of the best decisions the governor made."

At the parole board, the wheels have been turning very slowly as regards Abdur-Rahman. The board must make a recommendation to the governor on every proposed commutation. In Abdur-Rahman's case, the process leading to a recommendation was initiated by the board itself, which usually means the recommendation that will go to the governor will be a favorable one.

Abdur-Rahman was visited by an official of the board in September 1987. It was not until November 1988 that the board voted to go on to the next step, a public hearing.

Last March, board chairman Hudson told me letters would be sent to the prosecutor and sentencing judge at Abdur-Rahman's trial, preparatory to the scheduling of a public hearing. He estimated then that the board's recommendation likely would go to the governor in "six or seven months."

But a check with the board this week indicated those letters still have not been sent. It was not possible to ascertain why. Such foot-dragging is extremely discouraging to Abdur-Rahman, who has been waiting anxiously for his public hearing for nearly two years.

Whatever the board's eventual recommendation, the governor is free to ignore it, and with society in a thoroughly punitive mood, an anti-commutation stance plays well politically. The Abdur-Rahman case is an opportunity for the governor to demonstrate that his commitment to fairness transcends such concerns.

Commutation, after all, is a legitimate part of our justice system and warrants the same case-by-case, individual-by-individual consideration that reigns in our courtrooms. A blanket refusal to commute can be cruel, killing the hope of the deserving few, and ultimately subverting the concept of rehabilitation.

Truly dangerous prisoners lucky enough to have received parolable sentences are regularly released from the overcrowded prisons, only to rob, rape, and deal drugs again.

Yet a man like Abdur-Rahman is left to languish, even though he has long since paid his just debt. Even though he would be not a threat, but a contributor to society.

His continuing incarceration is a greater crime than any he committed.

Golf Has the Green

In the past I have been accused, usually by people in extremely color-ful pants, of being "anti-golf," which has come to carry almost as much emotional censure as "anti-American" did during the Vietnam War.

But I'm not anti-golf. I'm just pro-bowling.

Bowling and golf have a lot in common. Both are nonathletic skill games that can be played by almost anyone (though mastered by relative-ly few). Both are ideal activities for senior citizens.

Bowling is the more popular. About 70 million Americans bowl, roughly three times the number who golf. Also, more people watch pro bowling on television than pro golf when the two go head to head in the same time slot.

The Masters golf tournament in Augusta, Ga., for example, is consid-ered the most prestigious event on the Professional Golfers Association tour. CBS, which broadcasts the Masters, has promoted it in reverential tones as "A Tradition Like No Other."

Yet on Saturday, April 7, from 3 p.m. to 4:30 p.m. when the "Tradition Like No Other" had to compete against ABC's broadcast of a pro bowling tournament in Indianapolis, it finished second. About 3.6 million homes were tuned in to the ballyhooed Masters. About 3.8 million preferred good old bowling.

This happens all the time. During the first quarter of this year, ABC says, its bowling tournaments got larger Saturday audiences than 10 of the 11 golf tournaments on CBS and NBC. Nonetheless, the typical pro golf tournament is given 6½ hours of network airtime and the typical pro bowling event but 90 minutes.

Why is this so?

Because advertisers want as much time as possible with the audience that endures the Wagnerian tedium of televised golf. That audience is not only low on independent imagination, it has lots of money. The bowling audience, meanwhile, is presumed to be a bunch of schlubs hard to stimulate to artificial appetites. My kind of people.

The growth of golf in the last decade is a great commercial success story for land developers and sporting goods companies. It's a masterful exploitation of people's desire to live, even if just for a couple of hours a week and at considerable expense, as they imagine country-clubbers live. No wonder that Ralph Lauren, who made a fortune off people's readiness to emulate advertising images of landed gentry, has produced a line of golf clothes.

The gullible print media, of course, can't resist the haunting wail of the money train. They virtually ignore bowling but assign battalions of reporters to minutely chronicle pro golfers as they flit from artificial landscape to artificial landscape. Sports Illustrated recently ran a breathless, interminable series of articles on the "golf boom," including an illustration depicting the map of the United States as a gigantic putting green. A lucky thing for SI it didn't extend its giddy graphic metaphor to Canada. Not long after, a police officer in Quebec was killed as Mohawk Indians defended a sacred burial ground against encroachment by a golf course.

Yet, though the golf equipment sales rise, and the designer courses with names like amusement park rides proliferate, and the greens fees go up, up, up, more people still prefer to go bowling.

Bowling is inexpensive. It is communal. It does not deform vast stretches of landscape. Its tradition is big-bellied, big-hearted, small-d democratic.

Over the next few days, the media of Detroit, America's premiere bowling city, will be swooning extravagantly over the Buick Open golf tournament in Grand Blanc.

You'll have to look hard to find reports of the Quality Inns International Summer Bowling Classic from Edmond, Okla., though it probably will be watched by more people.

To the money interests, however, those people just don't matter.

Maybe it's their clothes. Maybe what bowling needs is Ralph Lauren. Put a couple of his pale-eyed, square-jawed Aryans on the lanes in tweedy smocks embroidered with "Butch's Better Drain Service," and just watch the perceptions change.

Lost Wilderness

The two-seater airplane banked and shuddered in a strong wind over Anchorage as the pilot summarized his thoughts about Alaska and oil.

"I can tell you right now," he said, "that if we sell our birthright to this thing, we will have made a tragic error."

It was June 1975 and scarcely 16 miles of the 799-mile trans-Alaska oil pipeline had been built. The pilot was the state official in charge of ensuring that construction of the pipeline did not violate Alaska's environmental protection rules.

His name was apt, Charles Champion, and despite his misgivings, he was confident Alaskans could have their oil and their singularly pristine habitat, too. "We have the know-how, the ability and the desire to see that our future is handled cautiously, prudently and properly," Champion told me that day. "This is an opportunity for the state to prove what we can do."

Since then, 14 years have passed. Almost seven billion barrels of crude have crept down the pipeline, $20 billion into the state treasury.

And today, near the pipeline's southern terminus at Valdez, sea otters freeze to death because the insulating quality of their fur has been destroyed by oil from the worst tanker spill in North American history. Bald eagles eating the carcasses of oil-killed water birds soon will die as their own intestines become coated. The herring harvest in once-crystalline Prince William Sound has been canceled, and fishermen work furiously to save the vital San Juan salmon hatchery. A refrigerated tractor-trailer in Valdez will store corpses of wildlife for future litigation.

Almost a quarter of a million barrels spilled. More than 1,500 of Prince William Sound's 2,500 square miles covered with a dark, clotting slime.

It is as though Alaska has hemorrhaged.

Meanwhile, 799 miles away on the fragile North Slope, the tapping of the state's artery at Prudhoe Bay proceeds in an ecosystem so delicate, pipeline builders were prohibited from spraying to kill the fierce mosquitoes. The insects torment the caribou, keeping the beasts moving and preventing them from overgrazing the sparse vegetation.

Today the North Slope is black-and-blue from chemical spills and waste leakage inflicted by the companies taking the oil.

We are far from Alaska, most of us, and don't know from sea otters. We do know about our Hondas' and Pontiacs' hunger for gasoline, however, and care a lot about the little numbers on the self-serve pumps. Most of us live in places long since fouled by the by-products of the good life. Poisoning, we accept, is the handmaiden of prosperity.

Yet, if Alaska is just another pollutable place, something is gone from the national sense of self. Alaska has long been a presence in the American mind: the last, vast expression of the wilderness so necessary to our national myth and character.

As long as the oil was kept out of sight in pipeline and tanker, psychological Alaska remained intact.

Now, however, that sullen lake of crude oil drifting toward the Gulf of Alaska, sullying entire islands, sullies also our schizophrenic hope that — cautiously, prudently, properly — we can keep special places safe from our pursuit of ease. Bitter evidence the Alaskan birthright has been sold, the tragic error made.

Educated to a Fault

One of the surest ways to get a rise out of my kids is to bring up the subject of Japanese education.

Forks plunk down on dinner plates, arms fold defiantly, chins jut. "I don't care how smart Japanese kids are," one will say. "I'm not going to school on Saturdays and I'm not going to school all summer, either."

I admit to having on occasion flogged my children to their algebra books with the specter of fanatically diligent Japanese students laboring far into the night on the other side of the world ("they're so far ahead in math and science, your whole generation may end up working for them"). I bet I'm not the only American parent who's done this.

Increasingly, however, I admire my kids' resistance to the comparison. They don't want to be like the Japanese and, to be truthful, neither do I.

Despite Japan's admirable achievements in science, technology and industry (nowhere more appreciated than here in Detroit), life in that country is painted in rather gloomy hues by Westerners who live there. It is overcrowded, overstressed, overexpensive, over-regimented, racially arrogant and lacking in imagination.

Japanese children are fed to the beast as soon as they enter the educational system, a ruthless winnowing designed to produce a magnificently credentialed few. Those eliminated at each step are condemned to spend their lives in a corresponding socioeconomic niche. The American journalist James Fallows, who has lived in Japan for three years, notes that "even now, the commanding heights of Japanese business and government belong to those who did best on university admission exams."

Such rigidity is as foreign to American tastes as whale meat. Our educational system, for all its flaws, seeks to catch up and lift as many as it can. Consider: One of every 19 Americans is in college, one of every 50 Japanese. Such a full net is admittedly a lot harder to hoist to great heights. But it is designed to exclude as few as possible, to give as many people as many tools as they can handle for taking advantage of the more numerous opportunities a flexible society offers. Unlike Japan's, our concept of mass society incorporates individuality, self-determination, redemption — the idea, as Fallows says, "that people could keep having second chances until the day they die."

I don't think we want to abandon this just to regain an edge in the semiconductor business.

Practically all the claims I've heard of the superiority of Japanese education center on that country's great industrial success. But industrial success is not the only success.

I am not educating my kids to be more precisely calibrated, smoother functioning parts in their nation's economic machine. I am educating them to extract the fullest measure of joy from their lives. To be competent and useful, yes. But also to value freedom and individuality, to control their own fates, choose their own loves and be capable of loving them.

Such things can be learned in no math or science book I know of, no matter how many hours a kid puts in. They grow up in the leisurely spaces between the tasks of youthful scholarship, where there is time to think, to interact with family and peers, joy-read, daydream, loaf, achieve a sense of self.

Two days a week and three months a summer seem barely time enough.

Look Here, Toots

Lately, feedback from readers has indicated I'm getting a reputation for being, well ... sensitive.

Mr. Sensitivity — the high-priced condom of newspaper columnists. What terrible timing.

Four tough guys named Rehnquist, Kennedy, White and Scalia, plus a gal (it's probably OK to call her that) named O'Connor, have just OK'd the reinstitution of men's suzerainty over women. Watch next year as male state legislators stumble over one another to pass restrictive new abortion laws.

A chill wind blows, and it smells of undiluted testosterone.

My problem here is my writing style. Too circumspect. Too fearful of offending. Recently I've been thinking of adopting the more macho style of Robert Leslie Bellem, a detective-story writer who died in 1968.

Here, for instance, is my Bellemesque column on the Supreme Court abortion decision:

The long black bucket she'd sent over dropped me off at a back entrance to the courthouse. Two slit-eyed dicks took their sweet time checking out my ID. I lit up a gasper and exhaled impatiently; finally they led me up the marble staircase.

The O'Connor quail was waiting for me in her office. I copped an appreciative gander. She was a gorgeous little taffy-haired morsel, dainty as a Dresden doll in a combed wool ensemble. She ankled across the carpet, sparklers gleaming on each ear, lamped me for a moment and extended a hand. I gave her my flipper.

"So nice to see you," she purred. "Journalists don't often get up here."

"Neither does progressive thinking, Toots." I spewed smoke from the corner of my mouth. Her tempting crimson kisser drooped miserably.

"Oh, why is it you reporters can't understand the pressure we're under? Bush. Falwell. Gingrich. ... " Her blue glims puddled with brine.

Just then I felt a presence behind me. I wheeled around to find a sawed-off, blue-cheeked bozo about to dole me out some knuckle tonic. I blocked his meat hook and let him have one in the tripes. He gasped like a leaky flue and fell flat on his smeller. For a second, I thought I'd corpsed the guy. "Who's the gorilla?" I asked.

The O'Connor doll went pale around the fringes.

"Antonin, Antonin," she cried. She knelt beside him and took his beardy cheeks in her sweet mitts.

The Scalia lug came around and fastened the sour scrutiny on me, like a guy with stomach ulcers contemplating a dill pickle. I felt like dealing him a bop on the attic for good measure.

"Complain all you want," he yelled, foaming at the yapper. "Women's control over their own bodies is DEAD! DEAD AS CANCELED POSTAGE!"

The O'Connor tomato rose and faced me. Her face had gone hard. She had a gat in her duke the size of a fowling piece. I lamped the roscoe nervously.

"Get out," she snapped. "I don't know why I ever let you come here."

I flipped my gasper into a corner and straightened the brim of my hat. "I know why, kitten. Guilt. You wanted to make a confession. You wanted someone to forgive you."

The Scalia lug had struggled to his wobbly gams and was smoothing his suit coat. "This ain't the end of it, neither," he growled as I passed him.

I went down the stairs slowly, thinking, "Roe's a goner. And so is Wade."

It's Tough at the Top

Today we're supposed to reflect on those who hold sway over our daily strivings for income and self-respect, especially income.

It's tempting but too easy to discuss Boss' Day in terms of chain gangs, Captain Bligh, galley slavery and so on. That doesn't mean we have to talk about what's good about bosses, of course, but we can at least ponder what's difficult about being one.

Having done some hard time behind those walls myself — four years for the felony of misplaced ambition — I'm a little con-wise to the subject.

Typically, you rise to initial bossdom from the ranks. Within a month you suspect that the human wear-and-tear of supervising recent coequals may not be worth the 8-percent pay differential.

You may start out trying to be a small-d democrat of a boss who inspires comradely affection and leads by fraternal example. This, however, works only in Soviet propaganda films about World War II. In real life, subordinates make a fundamental distinction between order-giving and order-taking. Woe is the boss who does not take a similarly realistic view.

Bruised, you may then retreat into an embittered authoritarianism in which your principal explanatory communication with subordinates consists of, "Just do it." This does not work, either, because it inspires hatred. In most workplaces, there prevails an ultimate democracy in which subordinates "vote" by being either enthusiastic or recalcitrant. You will eventually be turned out of office.

The best approach is to be amiably distant yet subtly insistent on your authority, while keeping all job-related heartburn where it belongs, namely, concealed in the stomach.

In this state of equipoise, certain truths apply.

Between you and your subordinates there is an inequality of information about the workplace. When socializing with them, you must learn to bear their ill-informed fulminations about sensitive subjects while holding your tongue.

You cannot afford to be unguardedly expressive. Your every hiccup sounds like an earthquake to those who work for you. Squint too much during an allergy attack and some subordinate is sure to mistake it for a sign of ill will.

You become weary of coddling the egos of flamboyant, erratic underlings, and secretly fantasize about firing squads. You come to see in a new light those unassuming subordinates who accept tasks without protest and do them passing well.

The only colleagues you can afford to bare your soul to are other bosses (this is why bosses spend so much time in meetings among themselves).

You have to play a rigid game of team ball. Behind closed doors, you may dissent passionately from higher-ups' decisions, but you must face the troops with a look of sweet concordance. The higher-ups will judge you on how well you get the lower-downs to carry out the policy; you dare not let your half-a-heart show.

Hard time, I tell you.

If you're good, you get more money, more power, more momentous problems.

If you're lucky, you get paroled.

Bossing is properly the domain of the relentlessly secure, the unimpeachably mature and other habitual offenders.

Personally, I've been rehabilitated. You'll never see me in the slammer again.

Turn Tassels to Hassles

First, allow me to thank you graduates for inviting me to speak on such a momentous occasion.

Second, let me ask you: Are you really intending to go through life with those screwy haircuts?

Hahaha. Just kidding.

You know, back when I was finishing high school, commencement speakers talked a lot about the Future, a time when everything was certain to be better if we worked hard, stuck to our ideals and so on.

Unfortunately, I can't use that as my theme because my generation has by now pretty much used up the Future. Sorry about that.

This does not mean, however, that I can't offer you some inspiration.

For example, it will be the great patriotic achievement of your generation to pay off the national deficit we've run up. We expect nothing less. Your sacrifices in meeting this obligation will make us very proud of you.

Most of you probably have not heard of this deficit, although you know by heart the top 10 rock videos on MTV. That's because my generation replaced the notion of the Informed Public with that of the Entertained Public. It's a lot more fun, and we don't think it'll make much difference to our democratic way of government. If you discount the Reagan presidency, I mean.

My young friends, the world of work that lies before you is much changed from a generation ago. I'm afraid we've let that good old American industrial superiority kind of get away from us, and lost quite a few high-paying jobs for you. On the other hand, we've invented paper entrepreneurship, which has made a few people fantastically rich.

True, a lot of people have gotten poorer, but there's been enough affluence to spawn a whole new industry: consumption-oriented magazines. Many of you may find rewarding careers in selling them door-to-door.

As you prepare to begin your work lives, I recommend one virtue in particular: patience. You will find my generation clinging to all the best jobs for a long, long time to come. By virtue of our numbers, we'll make certain there are plenty of age discrimination laws enabling us to hang onto those nice salaries until the last possible moment.

And when we finally retire, you will have the honor and, may I say, sacred responsibility, of keeping the Social Security and Medicare mills grinding. This will not be easy. We recipients will greatly outnumber you providers. In retrospect, we may have been a bit selfish in not creating more of you to share this burden. But who wanted to trade video equipment and restaurant dinners for more diapers, if you know what I mean?

I suppose we might have eased things also by saving more of our money for retirement, but we've never been very good at that farsighted sort of thing. Bunch of Goodtime Charlies, I guess.

In closing, I urge you to look on the bright side of the world you are inheriting.

The coming ban on automobiles because of the greenhouse effect will ease a lot of traffic problems.

Your inability to own homes will relieve you of the tedium of yard work.

The AIDS epidemic will save you the time and bother of sexual self-discovery.

It is the duty of one generation to pave the way for the next. For that reason, you do not have to thank us.

It was our pleasure.

One Tragic Moment

On Wednesday, I went to Judge Hilda Gage's courtroom to see what retribution society demanded of Christopher Lowe.

Lowe, who is 22, was convicted July 18 of involuntary manslaughter in the death of James Axon, who had been a 19-year-old freshman at Western Michigan University. Axon died on a frozen Madison Heights parking lot after Lowe kicked him in the head following a 90-second fight between two carloads of young men.

The two groups had been strangers to one another. They'd exchanged insults driving north on I-75 in the small hours of last Dec. 30, then pulled off the expressway to settle things.

It had been a fool's fight, a beery, young man's fight with nothing at stake that mattered. It had taken place, as much as for any other reason, because no one had been willing to walk away.

Wednesday's proceeding in the crowded Oakland County Circuit Courtroom was a melancholy accounting of how much good had been confounded by a thoughtless instant of violence. Lowe, who is from Southfield, was brought in handcuffed and wearing blue, short-sleeve jail coveralls. He gave a long, nervous sigh as he lowered himself into a chair in the empty jury box, and leaned forward, elbows on knees.

In the first row of spectator benches, Ethel Lowe, Christopher's mother, sat with eyes fixed on him. Her face was a map of tension.

Ethel Lowe and two dozen relatives and friends had been waiting two hours and 20 minutes. They'd watched as the judge sentenced a parade of forgers, armed robbers, crackheads and thieves. Chris Lowe was not like them. He had been well brought up. He had a steady job, a lot of friends, and no criminal record.

His mother hoped Judge Gage would give him probation. His employer, P.C. Gage & Tooling of Sterling Heights, was holding his job for him and awaiting a call today. Ethel Lowe was prepared for worse, perhaps a year in the county jail with credit for time already served. At least he'd be home by spring.

Ethel Lowe and her friends were not the only interested parties present. On the opposite side of the courtroom, near the back, John and Sheila Axon, Jim's parents, also awaited the announcement of Chris Lowe's fate.

The Axons held no hatred for the Lowe family. After the difficult two-week trial, John Axon and Lowe's stepfather, Clarence Mathis, had embraced tearfully. The Axons did not hate Chris Lowe, either. They hated his act of violence, however, and wanted justice.

Assistant county prosecutor Pamela Maas spoke first. She stressed that Lowe "could have walked away" after the brief fisticuffs. Instead, he delivered the "vicious, malicious" kick. She urged the judge to imprison Lowe. "This court," she said, "needs to send a message that this type of behavior is not going to be tolerated."

After Maas, Sheila Axon addressed the court. The undercurrent of busyness and whispers in the courtroom abruptly ceased as the victim's mother read a prepared statement.

"On December 30th at 4 a.m., we received a phone call that all parents dread...." she began. "I felt like my head was going to explode. I could hardly get the words out to my husband that our baby was dead. We held each other and cried."

She and her husband and their three children were extraordinarily close, she said, and "now there is a tremendous void, an empty chair at the table."

Her voice began to quake; she brought it under control by speaking with somewhat more volume. "We have had the support of many good friends, but others shy away because they cannot deal with our pain.... It is painful to watch kids getting ready to go back to college. To hear of plans for a wedding or of the joy of a grandchild.... We invested almost 20 years in raising Jim and loving him. He was on his way to becoming a wonderful man.

"There are days when getting out of bed is a chore. We work, we pray, and we hurt. The pain at times is so great that even tears won't come to our eyes.... "

Sheila Axon asked that the maximum sentence be leveled. "Jim Axon is dead, and gone forever. Time in prison will not bring him back. But time in prison will say that Jim did live, and that it mattered, dying in an act of violence. It will send a message that ... we cannot tolerate this violence."

Silence hung in the air for several moments after Sheila Axon returned to her seat.

Then defense attorney Michael Sobel appealed to Judge Gage to place Lowe on probation. Chris, he said, had been gripped by "remorse and shock" from the moment he'd learned, two weeks afterward, that the young man he'd kicked had died. Lowe had already been punished enough. Imprisoning him with thieves and cutthroats "can only serve to enhance the total loss that has already occurred."

It was time for Chris Lowe to speak. He rose from the chair, his thick, strong hands bound before him; he seemed a young man more at ease working with them than with his tongue.

"I know I did wrong," he said almost inaudibly. "I've learned a terrible lesson.... " Here he sniffed and began to weep. It was several long moments before he could resume. "I share the grief of the family for Mr. Axon's death.... " Tears overcame him again. "But I ask not to be kept in jail any longer. I'll be punished all the rest of my life.... " He couldn't go on. He sat down.

Judge Gage spoke. She sounded weary and regretful. She had received 50 letters from people attesting to the good character of Chris Lowe and his family, and begging for leniency. She had received 30 emphasizing the Axons' loss, and demanding vengeance.

"What a terrible, terrible tragedy," Gage sighed. "One of those cases where a judge really feels drained. The defendant comes from a good home, a loving family.... The victim comes from a good home, a loving family....

"One tragic moment that everybody wishes could be taken back. In today's society, this is always happening. One tragic moment a trigger is pulled. One tragic moment a drunk driver goes down the street when he has no right to be driving...."

She was convinced, she said, that Chris Lowe would never again do anything like what he'd done in the parking lot. Yet his kick was a vicious act that required punishment. Before she announced the sentence, she noted that "the incredible thing is, the newspapers will publish it and the public will read the cold words, and nobody will appreciate the pain that the defendant's family is going through, as well as the victim's family."

State guidelines indicated a minimum sentence of between one and five years. The sentencing panel in the case had recommended a sentence of between two and 15 years.

Gage gave Chris Lowe five to 15 years in prison.

Ethel Lowe hung her head and pressed her fingertips to her mouth. Her husband put his arm around her. Friends rushed to console her. Chris Lowe was led away, looking stupefied. He stopped at the secured exit and gave a long, sad look to his mother. The door closed behind him.

Jim Axon is gone forever. Chris Lowe is gone for a long time. John and Sheila Axon's expectations of an intact family, Ethel Lowe's peace, these are gone, too.

Odd thing about violence: Let loose, it respects neither guilt nor innocence, right nor wrong. Ultimately, it takes everybody down.

Sending a message was a leitmotiv of the sentencing proceedings. The message, as articulated by Pamela Maas and Sheila Axon, was that society will not tolerate such violence as Christopher Lowe committed.

The only problem is, this society tolerates it all the time. Prides itself on its two-fisted, gun-happy mythology. Gorges on staged fights, murders and mayhem as entertainment.

Chris Lowe is guilty of his individual act. But society is guilty, too. Guilty of aiding and abetting violence, and of loving it more than a little. Culpable for not walking away in disgust from its promotion. Indictable for steeping our male children in how it equates with manliness.

Because we are guilty, we have been sentenced. Our sentence is to live in more fear than any other advanced people of what may befall our children and others we love when they are out of our sight.

MEN
AND
WOMEN

CHAPTER FOUR

Sincere SWM Seeks. . .

The November 1991 edition of Singles' Network has hit the mails, and, as usual, it's some of the most engrossing reading this side of Modern Demographics.

The guide contains more than 250 personal ads from the romantically challenged in the Detroit area. Perusing them is a lot more entertaining and gentler on the ego, not to mention hygienically more prudent, than trolling singles bars, I'm sure.

Even if you are not in the market for a relationship, it's reassuring to read of so many classy, fun-loving, intelligent, sincere, irresistible, trim, upbeat, affectionate, charming, voluptuous, sensitive, financially secure, old-fashioned, adventurous, gracious, fireplace-fixated people with terrific legs, used mostly for long, soulful walks.

Many of the ads in Singles' Network are intentionally quite funny: "... I dislike tobacco, the NRA, hypocrisy. (I can't stand beets; there's no hope for beets.)"

Others are humorous, although probably not on purpose, such as this from Beautiful But Down-to-Earth Blond: "You must be 6 feet or taller with straight dark hair ... single, physically fit, nonsmoker with secure job ... who loves wearing a suit, romantic dinners, dancing, WJZZ, travel and intimate time with one special person. Jewish men are also very encouraged to respond."

Reading the advertisers' self-portraits, it's hard to fathom how such magnificent creatures could have been overlooked by the imperfect rest of us. Could there be a major tragedy of human disconnection going on?

Personal ads, however, are not about honesty. They are brief, coded press releases, hooks baited with some pretty bits of personality. "Haiku of self-celebration," as essayist Lance Morrow has referred to them.

It would be refreshing, however, to read a personal ad that was really candid:

ROTUND, BOW-LEGGED, chain-smoking bass fisherman/handgun enthusiast, 30-ish but looks 50, currently between occupational opportunities, half-heartedly seeks, at nagging mother's insistence, woman who wouldn't be too much trouble and who owns fishing boat with good motor. Send photo of boat and motor.

OK, you'll probably never see an ad like that. The ads, however, could at least admit a little ambiguity:

PROFESSIONAL WOMAN, 35, blond-streaked to cover emerging gray. Never married. Not very pretty except inwardly. Most of the time. Hears biological clock ticking, but doesn't care to know the exact time. Likes tennis. Plays dreadfully. Finds lawyering not what it was cracked up to be. Sometimes thinks she seeks serene professional man, 34-50, nonsmoker, gourmet, arts lover, who can be catalyst for change. Who's she kidding? Could fall for roofer, if kindly and attentive.

SELF-EMPLOYED GENT, 48, in final throes (he hopes) of mid-life crisis. Lusts for life but often asleep in front of TV before "Cheers." World once his oyster, now looks more like zebra mussel. Alternately pleased with perspective of maturity and oppressed by intimations of doom. Keeps finding hair growing in ears. Wishes he could be 30 again. Would settle for patient, forgiving woman, 35-50, to remind him on bad mornings life is still worth a shot. Terrific legs a must.

Size and Whispers

Two medical supplies manufacturers have begun marketing condoms larger than the usual one-size-fits-all. I hope they realize they've set sail for some of the most troubled waters of the male psyche.

The new products are called "Magnum" and "MAXX," and were developed in response to a minority of men who complained that the standard size was uncomfortably small.

The MAXX, for example, boasts 1¼ inches beyond the standard seven, a wider sleeve and 25 percent more of what the manufacturer refers to as "head room."

Well, you won't find many guys who (will say they) aren't familiar with the condom-discomfort problem. Most, however, have suffered in silence the industry's inadequacy in addressing their physical requirements.

The uni-size condom fostered a kind of psychic, small d democracy that helped obscure the jittery issue of comparative male dimension. A little physical discomfort, nobly borne, was a small price to pay for the serenity of the entire gender.

Oversize condoms, I fear, will prove the first step toward a complete range of sizes. Such a development will open the frail bird cages that barely confine males' sexual insecurities, which will then take panicky flight on wings of euphemism.

I mean, imagine a man taking his purchase to the drugstore cash register, and the checkout clerk calling back to the pharmacist, "How much are the Extra-Small Trojans?"

No, manufacturers of sized condoms are going to have to devise a terminology as expansive as Magnums. To wit:

"I'd like some condoms, please, but I'm not sure which size."

"You mean Jumbo, Gargantuan, Leviathan or Colossal? Gee, I don't think I can advise you."

"What size did that fellow you just waited on get?"

"Gargantuan."

"Well, then you'd better give me Leviathan, miss."

The old, nervous, comic-opera preoccupation lives on, gloriously immune to the appeals of reason.

Medical researchers, who are probably pretty exasperated by now, have been telling us for years that size is negligibly important to a man's ability to sexually satisfy a woman, which is, after all, the consideration at the root of all this.

For a variety of physical reasons, they instruct us, women don't much care about the size issue. It is moot.

Yet, in the vain and fearful psyches of men, where worries about sexual performance muddle in a smoky, bubbling cauldron with athletic achievement, defeat, victory, it remains a thing of animalistic myth and legend.

So sensitive a subject is it that the Masters and Johnson Institute, which discusses almost every other aspect of human sexuality with stupefying candor, refuses to release its research findings on average dimensions, observed extremes and the like.

In the past, the institute has learned that too many men find such cold intelligence distressing. As uncomfortable, say, as having to ask the pharmacist's clerk for a "Junior."

Love in the Fantasy Booth

The faces on the magazine covers seem to float detached above the bodies. White, black, Asian, Hispanic, male, female, they are transfixed in stagey looks of wonder, pretending delight or sultriness or ecstasy. After a while, they are more interesting than the contorting, combining anatomies beneath them.

The whole place is a kind of wonderland; its atmosphere is clean, cool, disconnected from reality.

There are films and books and videocassettes, and dozens of one-seat closets where a quarter buys a minute or so of full-color videotape depicting every amalgam and multiplicity of coupling humans.

A wall hung with supple plastic devices, outsized things with anomalous bumps and riflings, looks like the prop department for a film about space aliens. Every so often, a feminine voice, stewardess-like, chimes over the public-address system, announcing that Blaze or Paris or Launi, having finished her dance in the small inner theater, is now available in booth number such-and-such "for your entertainment pleasure."

And the dozen or so customers in the Park adult entertainment center in Lincoln Park on a weekday afternoon — the well-dressed older man who drives the huge luxury car parked in the lot outside, the younger fellow who owns the dented sedan with the child seat in the rear and the yellow "Baby On Board" sign in the window — wonder: Do I dare?

The booths are advertised as "private fantasy booths," and there are a half dozen or so. Some are only for candid talk; others are for "sex education." They are clean and brightly painted and the ultimate expression of prurience's contradiction — the simultaneous stimulation and impoundment of the love drive.

For the Park seems a careful and well run wonderland. The management's determination to observe the law is apparent. Discreet security men escort the female staff from dancing runway to fantasy booth to rest room, so that customers cannot touch them. Patrons are admonished not to seek dates or offer money to the women for extracurricular activity; the vice squad, a prominent sign warns, visits regularly.

In a fantasy booth in the middle of the place, Blaze is available for one's entertainment pleasure.

"Hi," she calls in a muffled voice from the other side of a window hung with Levelor blinds. "Do you know how this works? Come in. I'll show you."

The customer enters a door to a cubicle in which there is an ordinary chair, a round ashtray, a wall-mounted telephone, a stainless steel Kleenex dispenser and a large wastebasket one-third full of crumpled tissues. The chair faces a clear glass wall, on the other side of which sits Blaze, in a leopard- skin bikini and black high-heeled pumps.

The compartment on her side of the glass is somewhat more oblong than the customer's, but not long enough for her to recline at full length. Her entire floor space is taken up by a short, raised mattress with a tiger-striped coverlet. To her right is the window with the Levelor blinds; to her left an exit door, above her a sign that says "Thanks For Asking, But No Dates Allowed."

Blaze is slender and small breasted and pale. Her shoulders are dusted with russet-colored freckles. Her hair color is red, her face sharp but appealing, her teeth slightly buck. She is 28 years old.

She picks up a phone on her side of the glass and points to the one on the customer's side. Her voice is clear and friendly, full of ease.

Depending on how much the customer wishes to pay, she explains, she does one of four routines. Five dollars buys disrobement and a limb-splayed pantomime of copulation; ten an even more intimate look; fifteen a display of self-manipulation. "For $20," she says in conclusion, "I get into heavy orgasm with my little friend here." She shows a white plastic tubular device.

The customer slips $5 through a small porthole into her compartment. "OK," she says. "Go ahead and lock your door."

With that, Blaze twists the blind closed, switches on a light that better illuminates her and takes off the bikini (but leaves the high heels on). She reclines, parts her knees wide, undulates her hips, licks her lips. Into the phone, which she holds with one hand, she makes noises like "rowrrrr" and "unh, unh."

Blaze does this work 7½ hours a day, six days a week. Her customers run the gamut from Mr. Lonelies to gays curious about the opposite sex, to married men who visit to get a running start on an evening of love with their wives.

Blaze manipulates herself a little with her free hand (crossing the line, at no extra charge, into the $10 routine), lifts her heels and props her legs against the glass partition, offering a different angle. There is a knock at the exit door behind her. She apologizes and opens it. One of the security escorts hands her a small paper sack. "My lunch," she explains. "A hamburger. We usually have to order out."

In a moment, she is making sounds in the phone again and flicking and massaging her body parts.

Talk to me, the customer says, about love.

"You mean making love?"

No, he says, just love.

Blaze stops and casts her eyes to one side and bites at the corner of her mouth. "I know there's got to be a lot of openness," she says, nodding thoughtfully. "Like if a friend tells a man something about his wife, he shouldn't just go home and jump all over her. He should ask and give her a chance to explain. And it's no good having secrets. If a woman cheats on her husband, say, even if he never finds out, she's got to carry the secret, so there can't be that openness."

"Love ought to be a mutual thing," she says, gesturing back and forth with half-closed hands as though she and the customer on the other side of the glass were the lovers in question. "There ought to be a lot of give and take."

She falls silent. Blaze and the customer sit peering at one another through the glass barrier, the phones dead in their hands.

Finally, Blaze smiles.

A funny request, she says. No one has ever asked about love before — not in the fantasy booth.

Lost in the Translation

No wonder those scholars cleaning up the Bible's act started with the New Testament. In retranslating the Good Book so it might be safely and comprehensibly read by 9-year-olds, they saved the hardest for last.

The new translation, called the Contemporary English Version, is being done under the auspices of the American Bible Society. The new New Testament will be ready this month, but it's going to take five more years to rework the Old Testament.

The scholars are probably going to need all of the extra time, too. Every kid fetched up in the Judeo-Christian tradition knows the Old Testament is where all the really good stuff is. You can just imagine what the scholars have been going through, for example, de-sensualizing the Song of Solomon:

"Ladies and gentlemen, I know we've all been dreading it, but it's time to take up the Song. Our Song subcommittee has assembled a list of particularly troublesome passages, and proposed new language suitable for children. We'll be interested to hear your thoughts."

"All right, then. Chapter 1, Verse 4: *We will remember thy love more than wine.* Not a good idea, we believe, glorifying alcohol consumption in this context. The subcommittee proposes: *We'll remember your love more than a nice, cold Dr Pepper.* Some members of the subcommittee preferred the phrase: a nice, cold 7 Up. The majority, however, did not want to provide an opening for the numerology cranks. Everybody knows how the 666 mark-of-the-Beast thing in Revelation got way out of hand.

"Next, Chapter 1, Verse 10: *Thy cheeks are comely with rows of jewels, thy neck with chains of gold.* A terrible example, the subcommittee believes, for children growing up in neighborhoods infested with wealth-flaunting drug dealers. We suggest the following language, instead: *You have rosy cheeks and that's a really awesome T-shirt, too.*

"Moving on to Chapter 1, Verse 13: *My well-beloved ... he shall lie all night betwixt my breasts.* The problem here is self-evident. The subcommittee suggests: *My friend is really neat; maybe he can sleep over tonight, if it's OK with my mom.*

"Similarly, Chapter 3, Verse 4: *I found him whom my soul loveth: I ... brought him into my mother's house, and into the chamber of her that conceived me.* We of the subcommittee worried a great deal about whether this could be construed as advocating teen sex at home when Mother isn't around. Our proposal: *I really liked this guy, so I brought him home and introduced him to my mom.*

"Let us turn now to Chapter 4, Verse 11: *Thy lips ... drop as the honeycomb: honey and milk are under thy tongue; and the smell of thy garments is like the smell of Lebanon.* The subcommittee was split on whether this could be read as inviting a lot of passionate kissing, or was safely incomprehensible. Both factions, however, agreed on the following replacement: *You have a pretty smile. Your breath always smells nice, too. By the way, did you just take that sweater from the cedar chest?*

"Chapter 5, Verse 4: *My beloved put in his hand by the hole of the door, and my bowels were moved for him.* A very, very difficult one. Is the reference sexual? Is it scatological? The subcommittee simply couldn't decide, so we give the full committee a choice. If it's sexual, we suggest: *We held hands and it made me feel good inside.* If it's not, we propose: *My friend flushed the toilet after I went to the bathroom.* For obvious reason, we're rooting for the first interpretation.

"Finally, Chapter 7, Verses 1, 2 and 3: *The joints of thy thighs are like jewels. ... Thy navel is like a round goblet which wanteth not liquor: thy belly is like an heap of wheat set about with lilies. Thy two breasts are like two young roes that are twins.* Frankly, the subcommittee is stumped. We were tempted to telescope all of this into: *You've got a terrific bod.* But, clearly, that wouldn't do, either. Heavens. Navels full of liquor, bellies like shocks of grain, breasts like either small deer or fishes' eggs (we can't figure out which). On this one we really must defer to the superior wisdom of the full committee."

Some Enchanted Evenings

What with the recent weather having turned the air into something like warm soup, I think more of you are now in the right frame of mind to accept the following truth:

There is nothing more inimical to romance between a man and a woman than sleeping together.

What I mean here is not lovemaking, but the idea of two noisy, humid corpora occupying the same confined space for the purpose of slumber.

Think of what happens to a person's status as romancer if while sleeping he is prone to boar-like snorting and drooling and inchoate noises reminiscent of a cartoon character. Or if sleep transforms her into a human space heater radiating sticky warmth over a 40-square-foot area in, say, mid-August.

At the root of this is the difference between romance and intimacy.

Romance is a way of overlooking. A kind of religion that grows up between two people; a sweet illusion blind to the baser physical evidence and focused on a shining ideal.

Intimacy, on the other hand, is fully seeing. When you're asleep, all kinds of physiological and mental processes are going on in you, and you have practically no control over their expression. You are an open book to whoever is in your bed and in the mood for some reading. The unguarded self is never more candidly on display. Sleeping together is the most intimate of human acts.

An excruciatingly scientific survey I conducted before lunch one day last week indicates a problematical state of affairs, inter-genderly speaking: In most heterosexual couples of long standing, the female apparently is more wed both to the concept of sleeping together and to the concept of romance.

I am sorry, but this is illogical.

According to the Better Sleep Council, women suffer more because of joint sleeping arrangements. They tend to be lighter sleepers. They're less likely than men to snore, and more likely to be wakened by snoring. They tend to weigh less, and are more vulnerable to the seismic disturbances caused by their partners' nocturnal tossings (an average of between 40 and 60 a night).

The council claims to know of women who sew golf balls into socks and attach them to the backs of their husbands' pajamas so that when the sleeping men roll to the snore-inducing face-up position, they're so uncomfortable, they roll onto their sides.

This is very touching, torturing one's beloved for romance's sake.

From this evidence, it would seem females have more waking time in which to contemplate their men in the state of sleep. To ponder their lip-smacking and buffoonish scratching and open-mouthed roaring at the ceiling and muffled, cretinous cries of alarm and imbecilic laughter (uh-HWUH, uh-HWUH, uh-HWUH), not to mention various eruptions of a digestive nature.

Absolute death, you must agree, to a dashing image.

The answer clearly is separate bedrooms. What could be more romantic than stealing into one's lover's chamber, cologned and fixed on an amorous purpose? Sales of dressing gowns and negligees would boom (although golf balls might dip a bit). Afterward, lovers would part, leaving one another with nothing more burdensome than fond, fresh memory to sleep with.

The sweet illusion would remain intact, and a fellow could still turn into Goofy for the rest of the night.

Mouth-to-Mouth

Valentine's Day is the one day of the year you're most likely to have somebody else's lips seriously in your face.

It's probably a good idea, therefore, for us to review together a few basic aspects of the theory and practice of kissing.

First, let's be clear about what these tips do not pertain to. They do not pertain to chaste little pecks on the foreheads of elderly parents. They are not relevant to boisterous, lipsticky aunt-kisses to the cheeks of cringing children (mmmMM-wah!). They have no bearing on ritualistic bussing by French military officers or Russian diplomats, or on the gestures of certain famously affectionate professional basketball players prior to tip-off.

No, the subject today is genuine romantic kissing. Kissing that, when it's hitting on all eight cylinders, transports the participants to a psychic realm filled with melting light.

This kind of kissing is a full-face exercise, involving the clever application, disengagement and reapplication, not only of lips but also of chin, jaw and, not infrequently, tongue. It also involves teeth, eyes, noses (and, in the case of some especially highly evolved people, mustaches). You need know only once the embarrassment of accidentally poking a kissee in the eye with your nose to grasp how important it is that all these elements interface correctly.

A word about eyes, the closing and opening thereof.

Over the years, advice columnists have sympathized with readers who complain that their partners kiss with open eyes. The columnists usually advise these people to lash the offenders with "What're you lookin' at, buster?" or "Take a picture, it lasts longer." Of course, the offended party has to open his or her eyes to know of the offense in the first place, and so is hardly justified in acting superior.

No matter what the Righteous Brothers said in "You've Lost That Lovin' Feeling," we don't have to worry about this question any longer. The new rule is, it's perfectly OK to keep your eyes open while kissing. It gives you the advantage of a certain detachment while maneuvering the other person toward that psychic realm referred to above. If both of you kiss with open eyes, the worst that will happen is you'll look cross-eyed to each other, which is always good for a yuk.

There are three kisses to avoid:

The Mechanical Engineering Kiss. This one is all torque and no tenderness. It involves a harsh initial affixing of one's oral orifice on that of the other party, followed by a powerful, mechanical chewing and sucking action of the mouth muscles. It gives the kissee the sensation of having become attached to an automatic milking machine.

The Mealy-Mouthed Kiss. With this one, all the tissues of the mouth go limp and slithery against the teeth, requiring the other party to engage in a kind of labial juggling act to collect enough matter in one place to get some leverage on. It is really murder if either party wears braces.

The French, or Soul, Kiss. You might still be eating breakfast, so I won't go into the slurp and humidity of this one. Suffice it to say that, as any retired Roman Catholic nun can tell you, it is a mortal sin each time you take part in it. Also, it has been known to cause teenage pregnancy, although not since about 1961.

Texas Tease

Hats off to new Dallas Cowboys owner Jerry Jones. Not only hats, but fringed vests, hot pants and white go-go boots, too.

Jones has proposed changing the Dallas Cowboys cheerleaders' uniforms, as well as the Calvinistic rules that govern the women's behavior. As a result, he is taking a lot of heat down there in Texas, where they like their half-naked women moral, if you know what I mean.

Whether Jones is aware of it or not, he has struck a blow for honesty, which is not something you'd expect from an oilman. He deserves our fervent support in this.

Indignant at the prospect of gyrating their butts in tight-fitting cycling shorts instead of hot pants, of bouncing their bosoms in halter tops instead of midriff blouses, 14 veteran cheerleaders late last week took their automobile-grille smiles right on out of the Cowboys ranch and headed for higher moral ground. The 23 newcomers on the squad are supposed to decide today whether they'll stay or leave.

Jones has proposed also to loosen policies that have kept the cheerleaders hermetically sealed from Cowboys players and from strong drink while in uniform. "There's no alcohol allowed around the cheerleaders ever," their former director sternly informed Jones when he and some other ole boys showed up at a rehearsal with beer in their possession.

The Cowboys have always been a little sensitive to charges the cheerleaders exist solely to sauce the violence of football with a little sex. The upshot of all these rules was that not even your average post-Arab oil boycott Texas millionaire, no matter how wide his real estate holdings, could hope to have a Cowboys cheerleader or two or three gracing the back seat of the new Eldorado.

This meat was strictly for lookin' at, podnuh. All real nice and moral like.

"It's always been a first-class organization that people would look up to," said cheerleaders director Debbie Bond, a resignee. "However, with the new regime of Jerry Jones, the high standards and principles that made the (squad) what it is today are about to be changed. ... It would be against my morals and my thinking to be a part of what it will be."

Spare me, darlin'.

The Dallas Cowboys cheerleaders originated the dance hall girl school of cheerleading that's become an inescapable part of college and professional sports. Not all their toting of American flags and visiting GIs and raising money for hospitals can obscure the fact that they exist first and foremost to sexually titillate.

Don't get me wrong. I'm as much in favor of sexual titillation as the next cowpoke, so long as we call it by its real name. It's the hypocrisy of the Cowboys cheerleaders that makes me laugh.

Invoking high moral standards to dignify the commercial display of female flesh is an absolute hoot. If morality were the cheerleaders' concern, they could volunteer for church work instead of putting their bods on exhibit for a pro football franchise (which pays them next to nothing).

With his Spandex cycling shorts and halter tops, Jones was just trying to update the tease. I mean, it's not like he was proposing G-strings and pasties with tassels on the ends.

We're not ready for that kind of honesty yet.

Kevin: Prince of Peeves

Oh, what is this thing women have for Kevin Costner, anyway?

Mention the man's name and a lot of otherwise discriminating females turn into warm puddles of drool. Is there something going on here that I'm missing? Me and 110 million other American males?

No, this is not envy. The fact that women are crackers over a movie leading man doesn't make him anathema to men. Men find most leading men as interesting to watch as do women. Practically every guy wanted to smoke a cigarette like Bogart and wear a tux like Cary Grant. Today, guys would love to have William Hurt's soulfulness or Harrison Ford's arch savoir faire. All of these actors convey the sense of a genuinely interesting personality beneath the makeup and scripted lines.

And then there's Kevin.

No matter the movie, he puts me in mind of a friendly, nice-looking guy who works in a hardware store. He delivers all his lines in the same flat, slightly whiny voice. His blandness leaps huge chasms of place, character and time. There's Kevin dressed up in a baseball suit. Now he's dressed up like a cavalry officer — no, wait, like an Indian brave. Oh, look — it's Kevin dressed up like Robin Hood.

Of course, James Stewart, Burt Reynolds and Gary Cooper have also been accused of playing themselves over and over again. But Stewart and Reynolds were funny, and Cooper kept his mouth shut a lot, which at least hinted at something interesting going on under his hat.

The other day, I saw Costner in "Robin Hood: Prince of Thieves." It was hard to concentrate, what with the women on either side of me salivating on my shirtsleeves. But from the moment Costner's Robin returned from the crusades and started making angels in the sand at Dover Beach, I had a pretty good idea what I was in for during the rest of the grandiose comic-book movie.

Kevin did not disappoint. Although ostensibly an English nobleman of the Late Middle Ages, he kept saying "fer" instead of "for," and "childern" instead of "children." A Robin Hood from, I think, Wisconsin. His acting style consisted primarily of being adorably at a loss for words for a moment, then swallowing his lines.

His status as female drool bait was acknowledged in the only T-and-A shot in the entire film. He is shown bathing nude beneath a waterfall.

But, ah, irony. The shot reveals Kevin's secret shame: His buns are as flat as the way he deliver his lines.

I don't think this alone will jeopardize Kevin's career. I'm sure we can look forward to more big-budget pictures with the K-man squarely at the center.

Personally, I wonder how he'd do Hamlet ("Uh, g-gosh, let's see. To be? Or, like maybe, not to be?"). I wonder how he'd do Capt. Queeg of "The Caine Mutiny" ("Well, I sorta showed, I think, you know, with, um, geometric logic that somebody musta taken off with all those strawberries ... ").

Most of all, I wonder how he gets all that time off from the True Value.

Tough Guys Don't Scramble

After this week's power failure, possessed again by the ghost of Robert Leslie Bellem (1902-1968), creator of legendary hard-boiled pulp-mag detective Dan Turner ...

My secretary Edna ankled into my office with a look on her sweet mug that made me think of half-digested canaries. Her blue glims sparkled from the candles burning on my desk and file cabinets.

"Whatcha got, gorgeous?" I said, leaning back in my swivel chair.

"Mr. Wallace P. Rendover, the head of the power company, is here to see you. I'll show him in."

I'd lamped more than one lug in a four-alarm fix, but none ever looked more wrung than Wallace P. Rendover. Fishbelly face. Lusterless orbs. He looked like a fugitive from his own funeral.

"Mr. Turner, you've got to help me," he began. "This power failure. We've worked night and day since the storm last week to fix the downed lines, but we can't seem to get the electricity restored to them."

"Yeah," I said, lighting a gasper from a candle. "I've noticed."

"Frankly, Mr. Turner, we suspect sabotage. Perhaps a man of your skills could get to the bottom of things fast." He took out a wad of geetus as thick as a paving brick and slid it toward me. "I believe this should more than cover your fee."

I copped a gander at the stack of jake. "God bless the public utility rate commission," I said.

Any private skulk worth his license could see Rendover's problem was an inside job. Next morning I was swilling joe in the power company cafeteria, studying the landscape. I was working on my 20th coffin nail of the day when a taffy-haired morsel pinned her seawater peepers on me and made with the come-hither swivel. She looked like she was electroplated into her green satin dress. I'd pasted the optic on many a tasty wren in my time, but this one took the cake and the muffins.

Straightening the brim of my hat, I got up and followed her. She led me down a series of stairwells to a dingy sub-basement, then disappeared around a corner. I smelled a rat. Unpacking my roscoe from its leather armpit rig, I stepped 'round the corner. Right then, somebody maced me over the conk, and I went down, my brain-bucket filling with fireworks.

When I came to, I was in a room of squawking telephones and blinking computer screens. Half a dozen desperate-looking people stood above me. I got up, straightened my hat and torched another gasper.

"So. The merry conspirators," I said.

A skinny twerp with a shirt pocketful of ballpoints stepped forward. "We knew you'd find out anyway," he said. "This is the communications center. We've been keeping the power off by scrambling the messages to the substations so they can't reactivate the repaired lines."

I lit another cancer stick from the butt of the first. "Yeah," I said. "But why?"

The kitten in green satin piped up. "Because it's better this way. Oh, Mr. Turner, do you realize what's been happening since the power's been off? With no refrigerators, people go to the store every day and eat only the freshest foods. There's no TV, so they actually talk to one another in the evenings. They go to bed early and make love. With no air-conditioning or streetlights and with the windows wide open, they fall asleep in perfect darkness. To the sound of crickets. Of neighbor kids camping out in the yard telling ghost stories. Oh, don't you see? This is all about quality of l-life. ..."

Her glims puddled with brine. She couldn't go on.

Do-gooders. I should have figured.

I thumbed my hat to the back of my head and rubbed my eyes. "All right," I said. "You knock off your little crusade and we'll call it even. I'll tell Rendover I came up dry. All he wants is the power back on, anyway."

I put my meat hook on the doorknob to leave, and thought of how appetizing Edna looked by candlelight.

"Just one thing," I said. "Give me a couple of hours before you restore the juice, OK?"

Pillow Talk, Talk, Talk

Ordinarily, I don't review books unless they are by personal friends who stand to profit from my gushing over them in print.

I made an exception, however, for "Secrets About Men Every Woman Should Know." Its title was just galling enough to make me take it on.

The maunderings of sexual self-help authors are something I roundly detest. For my money, they cynically exploit harried people's unconfidence about their own lives.

As soon as I laid eyes on "Secrets About Men Every Woman Should Know" (Delacorte Press, $17.95), I could guess what I was in for. It came in a dust jacket the color of after-dinner mints. Featured prominently on the front was a picture of the toothy, well-groomed author, Barbara De Angelis-comma-PhD. Not just your everyday blitherer, mind you, but somebody with a dissertation to augment her personal experience in the sack and creepy preoccupation with other people's love lives.

Barbara De Angelis-comma-PhD is a Los Angeles radio talk-show host and a contributor to Cosmopolitan. She wrote a recent best-seller with the chillingly fanatical title, "How to Make Love All the Time." According to the dust jacket of the new book, she is "one of America's foremost love experts." Right up there with Darryl Dawkins, the 7-foot basketball player who tells everyone he's from "the planet Lovetron."

The book, predictably, has many, many lists: The Six Biggest Mistakes Women Make with Men, the Three Biggest Mysteries About Men, the Ten Warning Signs of a Love Martyr, and so on.

My personal favorite is Men's Top 20 Sexual Turnoffs. Turnoff 3 is a good example of the helpful information that makes up the bulk of the book's contents. It is labeled, "Women Who Act Unfamiliar with a Man's Body."

Women should be aware, writes Barbara De Angelis-comma-PhD (who must not have been paying attention in English class when they covered the grammatical principle of number), that "men identify so closely with their penis that they interpret how you treat it as how you feel about them." "Many women," she admonishes, "have never really taken the time to get to know a penis." The solution: "Make friends with your partner's penis."

But how, oh how, to create this friendship? Barbara De Angelis-comma-PhD has the following suggestion for skittish women. She recalls, parentheses, exclamation point and all, the advice she gave a squeamish female friend whose lover was named Andy. "I want you to imagine that instead of being a normal person, your Andy was only six inches tall. ... The truth is that your Andy does have a 'Little Andy.' And it is only six inches tall (or whatever!). It's the essence of big Andy whom you love. And when you love that part of him ... you're loving Little Andy."

The book is preoccupied with oral sex. It's the New Oral Sex — that is, talk, talk, talk, talk, talk.

Have resentments toward old lovers that you fear you'll dump on your new lover? "Sit down with your partner and discuss your needs and expectations for your relationship."

Got a fellow who's hard to entice into the sack when his brain is still back at the office? "Talk with your partner about ways he can make a smoother shift from working mode to loving mode."

Got one who's more interested in having sex than making love? "I suggest you ... have a serious talk with him."

One who's able to express himself emotionally only through sex? "Talk about this pattern with your partner."

But beware Sexual Turnoff 17, "The Sexual Blabbermouth: Women Who Talk Too Much in Bed."

To successfully have the New Oral Sex with her man, a woman must keep in mind the Three Communication Secrets. Especially, Communication Secret No. 1, "Men communicate best when they have a focus for the conversation." She writes, to wit:

"Wrong way: 'Jim, I think we should have a talk about our relationship.'

"Right way: 'Jim, I think we should have a talk about our relationship. We've been dating for six months now. What do you think our strengths and weaknesses are, and in what direction would you like to see us go?' "

(I'd love to add the reply, "How about to a movie?")

As a paid-up member of the male gender, I can tell you I've encountered very few women in my life who couldn't see through me like I was made of glass. "Secrets About Men Every Woman Should Know." Hah!

So far as I'm concerned, what's ultimately wrong with Barbara De Angelis-comma-PhD's book is that its list of Men's Top 20 Sexual Turnoffs is one item short:

Sexual Turnoff 21, "Books that would transform the passionate churn of man-woman sexual relations into wordy exercises in self-analysis and self-improvement. Carnegie courses for the copulatory."

I swear, I'll have nothing to do with such imbecility again, and neither will Little Jimmy.

SONG
OF MY
OWN
SELF

CHAPTER FIVE

Me and My Handwriting

No, my word processor hasn't short-circuited, and neither has my brain.

I'm doing this for a reason.

Ever since learning to use a keyboard, I've gotten out of the habit of writing by hand. For more than two decades, I've typed just about every written personal communication, to insurance adjuster and dear old Mom alike.

I'm not kidding myself. I know why I choose to type. I might pretend it has to do with neatness and ease, but it's really a matter of self-concealment. The typed or written word expresses thought without revealing anything of the expresser's private hungers and shortcomings and what he or she weeps about when alone late at night.

Handwriting, on the other hand, is a direct assessment of the unmediated mind, a "casual encephalogram," in the words of writer Lance Morrow.

In his delightful collection of essays, "Fishing in the Tiber," Morrow wrote that "in longhand, the word is a differently and more personally styled object than when it is arrayed in linear file, each R like every other R.... (Typed) words march in uniform, standardized, cloned shapes done by assembly line." Handwritten words, however, "look like ragtag militia, irregulars shambling across the page, out of step, slovenly but distinctive." What the longhand writer sees on the page is "himself, all right."

So, enough of this hiding out. By writing in cursive, I'm giving you a chance to know me better, more subtly. I'm imparting not only thoughts, which have been carefully sanitized by self-censorship, but a little insight into the roily, odoriferous sewer of my subconscious. Hope it doesn't leave unsightly stains on the carpet.

What do these psychoneurological tracings say about the real me?

According to graphoanalyst Maxine Rede Tatters of Troy, the degree of rightward slant "indicates empathy; you really care about people." The raggedness of the right margin, however, is a sign that "you're a little apprehensive, as most men are. You're a little afraid of the future."

Luckily for me, I give great loop, both above and below the base line. Those below, on "g's," "y's," etc., indicate a healthy appreciation for the material and fleshly; those above, on "l's," "h's," etc., a taste for the imaginative and theoretical.

My "a's" and "o's" are very clear and clean — "There is no hanky-panky in them," Tatters says. This is a sign of honesty and straightforwardness. The same with my wide open small "e's," which show "you're very open to ideas and to other people, and that you're not prejudiced, either."

My small "m's," alas, are troublesome. Their bunched tightness indicates I'm a little repressed. "You're holding something back in your self-conscious." (I know what it is, too, but I ... just ... can't ... tell you.)

The major problem is indicated by a tendency to start the first letters of some words below the baseline. This can mean only one thing: resentment. "You apparently resent impositions on your time, or being tied down."

On the elaborate work sheet Tatters filled out on my handwriting, I scored high on precision, persistence, decisiveness, emotional responsiveness, and loyalty.

I scored low on positiveness, dignity, diplomacy, poise and the desire for responsibility.

More Dick Vitale than Alistair Cooke.

Myself, all right.

Avalanche of Memories

The road into the old town twists along the river at the base of hills as steep as melodrama. "Rock Slides," warn the signs.

Sandstone boulders rest on the shoulder of the two-lane. Driving past, you can't help but think that if one began its descent at just the right moment as you and yours were motoring in unlucky approach — well, scratch one homecoming. There would be a somber, entirely different reason for the aunts and the cousins to gather in the old town.

For a native son on a semiannual visit, the years condense crazily. The dead play peekaboo among the living. While the table is being laid for the family feast at my parents' house, I wonder if my brother-in-law's mother, with her high, pinched voice and fidgety ways, will be present. "Is Paul's mother still alive?" I finally ask. "She died years ago," my mother replies. "Don't you remember?"

The talk here tends to center on people who no longer exist. Not just the dead, but the robust young postwar parents gone frail, the babies now bald or menopausal. The future is spoken of in safe, small steps that skirt an abyss.

Abyss is endemic to the old town, what with the hills tumbling headlong to the river. A century and a half of the heaviest industrialization have not erased their somber grandeur. In fact, it is even more in evidence as the population thins to half what it was a generation ago, and demolished buildings create idle open spaces. The landscape imparts a subtle sense of jeopardy. Almost anywhere — between two dilapidating houses, or around the bend from the latest fast-food restaurant — you can be ambushed by a view of arresting sweep and depth. A person could fall if he didn't keep his back against the slope and his eyes on the abyss.

Sunday morning:

While the family is at church, I coax my father's great, floating old Oldsmobile through the shrunken streets of my childhood neighborhood. A cold blue sky falls away sharply on one side. The houses are narrow and cling to one another as though in fear of toppling down the slope.

The Italians who came to the old neighborhood were from a mountainous region. To them, there was nothing unusual about a house whose foundation began at the roofline of the house across the street. They scratched gardens into the level patches. Amid tomatoes and eggplants, the immigrant men pieced together small shanties, refuges from the child- and woman-filled dwellings a few paces away.

At the top of a plummeting hill, I pass my uncle's little grocery and butcher shop. It is boarded up. My uncle — brother of my father, husband of my mother's sister — smiles at me from somewhere, a thick-forearmed man in a blood-streaked apron who is long gone from the world.

I inch the Oldsmobile downward and come to the yard of the public school where I learned basketball. It no longer has a court. The school is no longer a school.

A few blocks away, I stop at the site of the old St. Anthony's grade school. The main building, a large, creaky, fire-baiting house built at the turn of the century, is gone. All that remains is the freestanding classroom where I attended first grade. Sixty kids, one Dominican sister of storied good humor. She picked me for the reading medal. Thus began my journey away from here.

A new St. Anthony's opened around the corner in 1959. Its name has been changed to All Saints, in embrace of other parochial schools that, as the population declined, were consolidated into it.

One of these days, I tell myself as I slip the gear shift into drive, I'll go to All Saints to hear the first-graders read. Do they still give a reading medal? Who will win this year's? What destination will be invisibly inscribed on it?

Next morning, I am up at 6 for the long drive back to where I am known only as an adult. Back to where the evocations are less profound and the dead stay put. We exit the old town as we entered, escaping the rock slides yet again, leaving the old folks up in the hills hoarding memories.

But My *Friends* Call Me. . .

In the last couple of decades, Chase Lake in Rose Township has come to be known as "Cheese Lake," a development that has definitely cheesed the people living nearby.

The township trustees, responding to the public discomfort, voted unanimously to ask that the Oakland County Board of Commissioners formally affix the name "Chase" to the lake.

It's easy to understand the residents' displeasure. When I think of "Chase Lake" I think of a body of water that's clear and clean ("chaste"). When I think of "Cheese Lake," I think of an exceptionally large amount of chip dip.

What applies to lakes applies also to people. The names they pick up in addition to or defiance of their given names inevitably affects how others perceive them.

Most nicknames are merely diminutives bestowed early in life by parents giddy with fondness (although I've got to wonder about the case of a boy I knew of named Richard Waggle, whose folks insisted he be called "Dickie"). Friends in early teenhood then knock off all the loving "ie's," transforming Debbies into Debs and Joeys into Joes. Nicknames that attach later usually are references to character, idiosyncrasy or obscure events in which a person participated.

The first law of nicknames is this: You can't do anything about them.

They stick or not completely independently of the efforts of namer and named. If you have a sobriquet you despise, you can rage against it till the very last person in Rose Township stops calling Chase Lake "Cheese Lake," but it won't do any good. Once a hated nickname sticks, your only recourse is to move to a place where no one knows you.

Certain subcultures have shown particular gifts for nicknaming: Italian-American gangsters (Anthony "Tony Ducks" Corallo, Carmine "The Snake" Persico, Simone "Sam the Plumber" DeCavalcante). Professional baseball players (Charles "Piano Legs" Hickman, Wilmer "Vinegar Bend" Mizell, Doug "Eye Chart" Gwosdz). My father's circle of old cronies ("Brownie," "Tuttles," "Peppy," "Doc," etc. — their monikers make them sound like an affiliate chapter of the Seven Dwarfs).

Scholars agree, however, that nicknaming reached its apogee in the person of William Lauder Hershey, late of Flint and now a Washington journalist. He is still known as "The Conqueror" to aging Sigma Nus from Albion College. At Flint Central High and then at Albion he bestowed or provided critical support for such sobriquets as "Naked Neil," "Hal the Hawk," "Tim the Toad," "Gary the Garbage Truck," "Tool" Munger, "Quitter" Greer, "Harry the Fish Merchant," "Man Mountain" McGrath and — his masterwork — Jock "Strap" Eufinger.

Hershey is the first person in history to have successfully nicknamed his own father (Clark "King" Hershey). To this day, the elder Hershey signs letters with a small drawing of a crown.

Hershey's name for me is "Clifton," the etymology of which there is not enough space on this page to explain.

Of course it's not the first nickname I've borne. At various times and to various people I have been "Jimbo," "Carlo," "Beak," "Rocky," "The Owl," "Banana Nose," "Magic," "Superstud" and "Einstein."

The last three, however, never stuck.

Getting out of Vietnam

Half an hour before sunrise, a thin, low fog clung to the rolling land around the Vietnam Veterans Memorial. Already there was considerable traffic on Constitution Avenue in Washington. Headlights sweeping through the stands of trees set the ghostly landscape in motion, igniting then extinguishing the mist, shifting and multiplying the shadows.

I'd come, at long last, to read the names. It was dark, but votive-like lights illuminated the black granite panels that make up the long wall of remembrance.

Since the wall was dug into this terrain 10 years ago, I'd been to Washington many times. Always, I found reason to not visit the memorial. Not having served in Vietnam, I did not fear the detonation of explosive memories of combat. My reluctance was based on a more general disinclination to scratch up old fears and angers that to me were synonymous with the war. Living with Vietnam's consequences — the destabilization of the economy, the end of our optimism — was plenty hard enough.

In 1969 and 1970, years of high casualties in Vietnam, I was a draftee private working as a speech writer and clerk in the Pentagon operation that assigned the Army's 1.3 million enlisted personnel. The heart of our operation was a vast expanse of clerks' desks, an ocean of bureaucratic tedium from which emerged tragedy for many thousands of families.

Names for the wall were designated first in our offices, then progressed from printed orders to melancholy telegrams home to, finally, black granite.

I'd gone to the memorial on the afternoon before the foggy morning. It was sunny and 70 degrees. Hundreds of people were there, queuing in front of the computer-printed books listing the names, and walking the wall's 496-foot length. Faces were somber. I saw one person with reddened eyes and nostrils, a middle-aged man who leaned forward on a bench as a woman wearing a wedding band stroked his hair. I walked the wall quickly, pausing a few times to peer over the shoulders of other visitors.

It was over in a few minutes, and I felt very little.

I decided to go back the next day, at an hour when I was sure to have the names to myself.

The books that list the dead are in lighted stands, glassed-in on all but one side. You reach beneath the glass to turn the pages, the bottoms of which are soft from fingering.

The names I'd had in mind I located easily:

Mastroianni, Thomas Francis, PFC, Marines, born 1 Sep 46, died 19 Mar 67, Panel 16E, Line 133. "Maz," my best friend when I was 10 and 11 years old.

Lulla, Robert Allen, 1st Lieut., Army, born 13 Nov 44, died 1 Apr 68, Panel 47E, Line 33. High school thespian, onetime seminarian. I remember him in a black turtleneck on the darkened school stage, performing a tortured existential monologue about religious faith, and crying out at one point, "Where are you, God? Goddamn it, God!"

Larkin, Thomas John II, Capt., Army, born 15 Aug 46, died 14 May 70, Panel 10W, Line 41. The son of a good friend of my father. A quiet, intelligent, red-haired boy I'd not known well. Sometimes one of his parents would stop their car and pick me up as I walked to school. They always drove him.

I'd heard that other names I knew might also be there, two college friends and some guys I'd gone to basic training with. These, it turned out, had eluded the wall.

I found the first three names and stood looking at each for a long time, but I couldn't say I felt the loss of them any more keenly. Alone with the names at this quiet hour, I still felt almost nothing.

The black granite began to reflect the lightening sky. Banks of clouds, underlit red, mounted behind the Washington Monument. I read the names of strangers, one after another, chanting them mentally, wondering if they'd have a cumulative effect. *Freddy Lee Sapp ... Sherman Chapman Jr. ... James R. Cumberpatch Jr. ... Antonio Murado ...* My contemporaries, somebodies' babies.

Nothing.

Maybe after all these years, I'm just grieved out about that war, emotioned to the point of deficit.

Also, there is an inarticulateness about the memorial itself. All those names, all that personal bad luck, but not a hint of the savage rifts the war tore in American society or the damage it did many who survived it or of how none of it needed to be. Those combat veterans whose pain drives them to seek, even now, a retrospective ennobling of the war, cannot take much comfort in the wall.

I hated to admit it. I don't think the memorial is going to prevent unnecessary wars in the future, and what else could have been its purpose? Already country-and-western singers crow boastfully about a new war to come.

"Twenty years," wrote John Kenneth Galbraith in a different context, "is normally the time it takes for the recollection of one disaster to be erased and for some variant on previous dementia to come forward."

Perhaps I'm forgetting, too, in spite of myself.

I arranged to go the next day to the Pentagon to revisit the place I used to work. I sought Room 1E609, the suite of offices where I'd manned my IBM Selectric. We were, in the Pentagonese of the time, "E-ringers," big shots whose offices were on the outermost of the five concentric rings that make up the building, and thus had windows that gave on actual daylight.

The Pentagon had changed. Although it still smelled of paperwork and tedium, although ubiquitous small fans still hummed against the poor ventilation in its countless cramped interior spaces, the place was quieter. More businesslike. Bereft of the swarms of low-ranking draftees, anxious bait for the dread "Vietnam levy" of my day. It was seedier, mechanically less reliable, two decades older.

The enlisted personnel operation had long since moved to a suburban office building elsewhere. New interior walls had been built and moved about. My guide and I determined the general area where I'd worked was now occupied by offices of the Army's inspector general and chief of engineers.

When we got to the place our best reckoning told us was the site of my old office, we found only a narrow hallway. It was completely unfamiliar to me. Next to a doorway closed off with drywall, someone had written "1E607" in blue Magic Marker.

1E609 was gone, reorganized and reconstructed into oblivion. It was as though it had never existed in the first place.

Up in Smoke

And so, in honor of this, my long-awaited anniversary, I rang up the American Lung Association and the Centers for Disease Control.

Where is my plaque? I asked.

Where is my certificate of guarantee, the one on stiff paper with an elaborate border, affirming that my biological future is very bright and very, very long?

On this day 10 years ago, I quit smoking. You needn't applaud. Lovely ladies in jogging shorts will pass among you for contributions toward a commemorative gift.

The smoking phase of my life lasted about 20 years; two decades of dramatic gesturing and youthful indifference to my own destructibility.

I started fooling with cigarettes in high school. The rules at our school banished smokers to the far end of a cement pavilion behind the building during lunch hour. We'd stand there in the sleet, ponderously drawing on our weeds and exhaling melodramatic proclamations of our addiction. *Aw, man, I was DYIN' for a smoke.* Those of us who played sports kept a nervous eye out for coaches.

In college I hit my three-fourths-of-a-pack-a-day stride. Cigarettes were not only a physical addiction but props, the artful manipulation and display of which were vital to the image of a guy who hadn't been around long enough to actually accomplish anything or form a genuine persona.

By the time I was 33, however, cigarettes' contribution to image had become less important than their impact on pulmonary tissue, the oxygen content of red blood cells, the width of arteries and the cancer-probability tables. I mean, a person actually could die, you know?

So on March 30, 1980, two friends and I sat down in a tavern and made a pact. We shot pool and smoked ourselves sick, and at midnight we stopped. I haven't restarted since.

Got out just in time, I did. Thereafter smokers were banned from airplanes, segregated in restaurants and chased from the interiors of entire vast office buildings. You see them now puffing their weeds in the cold outside the doors of banks and insurance companies. Adult delinquents banished, as in high school days, to the edges of the premises. Shivering, morose, vaguely threatening. An oppressed people.

When I quit, the literature, as I recall it, promised that in 10 years I could fully "pass" as a nonsmoker; that is, the likelihood of my being done in before my time became statistically indistinguishable from that of people who'd never smoked.

But when I called the Lung Association the other day, here's what a spokesperson told me: "Actually, we say that after about *20 years,* an ex-smoker's risk of premature death or lung cancer approaches that of a never smoker."

Shocked by this treachery, I tried CDC's Smoking or Health branch. "We have a study that says after *15 years* it's almost as though quitters never smoked," said a spokesperson.

So, the mothers went and changed the rules on me. After all I'd been through.

What can I do but regear my hopes for a longer haul?

I'll tell you what, though. If I make it five more years without coming down with something, they're not going to get off with some measly plaque or piece of paper. Nuh-unh. Come March 30, 1995, I'm going to be thinking statue, baby.

Pulling Punches

My defender fouled me (deliberately, I thought), and I flung the ball at him in anger.

The man brought his face very close to mine and said, "You can call the foul anytime you want, but throw the ball at me again and I'll break your arm."

He outweighs me by 45 pounds. Although he is older than I am, he is a fine physical specimen. Even his eyebrows, ominously bunched as they were just then, looked like they'd been trained on a weight machine.

"You know," I said to myself, "he's got a point."

I apologized.

This happened the other night during one of those athletic competitions marked by the kind of surreal fervor only the middle-aged can bring to them.

It caused some old, familiar discomforts to burn in my stomach: Had I been mature, or just cowardly? Had everybody else on the court been embarrassed for me? Had I gone down a notch in their esteem?

When is a man safely old enough not to fight?

I don't mean "fight" as in the heated exchange of legal briefs or the clash of career ambitions, but "fight" as in knuckles crunching against cheekbones.

Boys have to deal with this practically from the time they leave their mothers' arms and must begin divining who's the toughest kid in class, who can beat up whom, when you cry in response to a provocation and when you punch. As a rule, girls don't have to contend with such matters, and therefore think them foolish. That's probably why boys understand power at an earlier age (which doesn't mean they wield it any better at a later one).

Personally, I've hated fighting ever since I was little, and have always been willing to go to just about any length to avoid it. Fear of being hurt surely has had a great deal to do with it (although the humiliation of hiding or walking away isn't a lot less painful). But I've also felt civilization somehow tottering whenever I've seen a human fist slam into a human face.

Except for some mutual body-pummeling with my brother, I have never been in a real, two-sided fight, although I have taken a few punches, which is no chocolate sundae, let me tell you.

A part of me envies guys who feel differently, who are serene at the prospect of a fistfight, who can abandon themselves to the grim thrill of combat and welcome the clear-cut resolution it brings.

I was rather counting on full maturity banishing the need to worry about all this, but it looks as though the issue is going to surface and resurface on its damnable tide of testosterone right up until my creaky senescence.

So, at 42, I still sometimes fantasize about being lethal and rock-fisted, a decent sort who, when pushed to the limit, can expertly rearrange another man's physiognomy.

Identifying that limit — that insult or calling-out that can be answered honorably only with a roundhouse right — is the problem. Is it when another man calls me wimp, sissy, pantywaist in front of my son?

I don't know. Besides, I don't have a son.

And I can just see my teenage daughters rolling their eyes in exasperation at the sight of me squaring off with some other girl's dad.

Inner Problem Child

I couldn't deny it any longer. The latest wave of self-help psychologists finally got me to accept the truth:

I have an Inner Child. An instinctual, freely emoting little bugger I've ignored my entire adulthood.

You can't imagine the wild herd of questions that rampaged through my mind when I realized this, or the guilt, doubt and inadequacy it stirred up.

What if, during my long night of skepticism, something terrible had happened to him? What if he'd been hit by a car while too little to cross the street by himself? What if he'd died of starvation? Was I guilty of Inner Child abuse? If he'd survived, might he need orthodontia? Could I claim him as a deduction?

First, I had to find him.

I set out on foot through the dark, rain-slicked streets of my inner being, hoping I wouldn't find him in a girl's dress, or behind some closed door playing with himself.

My feet took me to the docks, that dingy quarter of myself that borders the roily, inky sea of my subconscious. The sound of a choir in ragged song came from a tiny church whose candlelight glowed behind a single stained-glass window. I recognized most of the small congregation, a few of my Better Impulses, several of my Altruistic Instincts.

But, no, they hadn't seen my Inner Child.

Closer to the water, I came upon a tavern. It was dimly lit, garishly painted, filthy. Weird music swooped above the patrons, who talked in low voices, ducking their heads in and out of the smoky shadows. Oh, I knew them. In the back booth, a couple of my Sexual Fantasies lounged lasciviously. Alone at a table, fidgeting and chain-smoking, sat one of my Major Insecurities. Three of my Crueler Tendencies snorted and guffawed at the bar.

I cringed at the thought my Inner Child might have fallen into such company.

But, again, no one had seen him, although the Sexual Fantasies made lewd faces at the prospect.

I walked to the waterfront. There I found him, leaning against a weakly glowing street lamp, playing with a penknife.

His hair was tangled. His clothes were tattered and his feet bare. His smudged face was set in a look of defiance.

He knew who I was, all right.

"I ... I'm sorry," I blurted. "But I'll make it all up to you. I swear."

He only smirked.

"What I'm saying is, I want us to spend real quality time together. We'll go for ice cream. I'll take you to the ballpark, to Inner Children's Palace."

I knelt and reached out to touch his hair. He brushed my hand away.

"Please," I implored. "We belong together. We're part of the same ... *personality*. We'll move into a nice house in a better part of my nature. You can have other people's Inner Children sleep over all the time. Oh, don't you see? I just want to be *in touch* with you."

I could sense the calculating going on behind his big brown eyes.

"You mean," he said, "I go with you and I get whatever I want?"

I hesitated. "Uh ... "

"I can stay up late, throw tantrums when I don't get my way, eat candy till I throw up, and you clean up the mess without complaining?"

"Well, I wouldn't go quite ... "

"I can bully weaker kids? Smoke cigarettes? Pull the wings off flies? Set anthills on fire?"

"Now, wait a minute, kid."

"What's it gonna be, Babycakes? My way or ... " — here he jabbed a forefinger at my head — *"therapy?"*

He leaned his back against the lamp pole, half smiling, and began cleaning beneath his fingernails with the tip of the knife. "You think it over, Pops," he said without looking at me. "You know where to find me."

I walked toward the beckoning daylight of otherness, newly eager for the external world. Other people. Other places.

I thought, "The hell with that little brat."

Berlin Unwalled

When I was 22 and an intern at a West German newspaper, I made the obligatory trip to the Berlin Wall.

On a raw, leaden day in fall 1968, I climbed an observation platform not far from Checkpoint Charlie. I could see the East German guards in their towers and fancied they were watching me. I imagined sprinting westward across the no-man's-land with their binoculars and rifle sights trained on my back.

No one else was on the platform. I wanted a souvenir but was a little apprehensive about taking one. The guns, the dogs, the tank traps, the monstrous masonry itself made for an unrelenting sense of forbidden-ness. Maybe souvenirs were forbidden, too. As inconspicuously as possible, I bent a six-inch length of barbed wire back and forth until it snapped off in my hand.

To me and others of my generation, the Berlin Wall divided more than Berlin. It was the palpable setting off of this side from "the other side." "Da drueben," ("over there") as the West Germans called it, was a kind of anti-world where, I'd been taught since childhood, untruth and evil prevailed and threatened to slosh over to engulf us all.

The wall ran along Bernauerstrasse, but also straight down the center of our psyches.

The sight of people now disregarding it — dancing on it — is to me a boggling of images akin to being drunk or experiencing religious conversion.

The division that the wall symbolized always has been a presence in my life, a matrix for thinking. It was a cause I officially served.

The year I climbed the wall, I also visited East Berlin. It was a dour place of unanimated people. The walls of its buildings were still pocked with bullet holes from the great Russian siege of the city during World War II. It was so unlike West Berlin, which had cleared away the rubble and set glittering new buildings in its place. West Berlin with its audacious nightlife and heavy concentration of gays (West Berlin residents were exempt from service in the West German military). Its wisecracking blue-collar workers, the Brooklynites of Europe.

Hopelessness and lethargy and physical neglect came to be identified in my mind with the city on the other side of the wall. The first time I saw Detroit's Monroe Block years later, I thought, "East Berlin."

Less than two years after my internship, when I was in the Army, I found myself trying to sleep in a rainstorm beneath a topless Jeep in the misty highlands of Hohenfels in eastern Bavaria, not far from that symbolic extension of the wall, the Czech border. I was alongside another soldier, and the Jeep wasn't wide enough for both of us to lie lengthwise underneath. So we lay crossways to keep our heads and upper bodies dry and gave our lower bodies to the rain for the night.

Although members of the easternmost U.S. combat unit in Europe, we were public information specialists from headquarters, not line soldiers who knew how to gear themselves for the elements. We were there to do a story on our unit's armored cavalry troop, which had the worst duty in the unit. It was "in the field," patrolling the border eight months a year.

The Vietnam War was going on then, but Europe was still the site of the ideological fault line along which the intercontinental ballistic missiles pointed at each other. Vietnam was where you could get killed. Europe remained the place where the world could get killed. All it would take was our cavalry troop spotting a column of Soviet tanks crossing the border from Czechoslovakia into Bavaria.

My fellow typewriter jockey and I discussed this most of the night, inasmuch as it was hard to sleep with cold, drenched legs — my most memorable bit of suffering in honor of the world's great disjunction.

Just as the wall symbolized that division, its present flouting is the ultimate emblem of the closing of the fault, which has come with such breathtaking ease this year.

Poland, Hungary, the Soviet Union and East Germany are embracing the ways of this side of the wall. Our side has won.

Uh, hooray.

But what are we supposed to do with this arsenal we've amassed over the last half-century? With this comforting way of thinking about the world and our country's importance in it?

Maybe now — faced with a united European economy that will be bigger than ours and a former Soviet adversary more interested in VCRs than MIRVs — we're to become peaceable. Perhaps we'll take the resources that have been drawn off for so many decades to man the wall — literally and figuratively — and apply them to the human needs at home. The need to make up ground in the education and character formation of our kids; the need to guarantee the security of our older people, our ill and our economically displaced.

Maybe we should send a delegation to dance on the wall, too.

Recently, I went looking among my memorabilia for the piece of barbed wire. Scrounging around the stuff boxed in the basement I found newspapers and letters and photographs from those days in Germany. I can't find my piece of the wall, however, and to tell you the truth, I don't miss it a bit.

Crashing the Market

A few months ago, I finally became a capitalist. Possibly there should have been a ceremony.

I am not the sort of person who rushes into,things, and wanted to make sure this capitalism stuff wasn't a fad invented on the back of a cocktail napkin by some *wunderkind* economic theorist. (Remember the Laffer Curve? Ha. A laugher, all right.)

This doesn't mean I ever believed in capitalism's onetime arch rival, Stalinist state socialism. All you had to do was look at the awful men's suits that system produced to know it was headed for the dung hill of history.

My entry into the stock market didn't exactly set analysts on the Street atwitter. Basically all I did was sign up for the employee stock plan at work. My older daughter graduates from high school in a couple of months, and I figured it was time to start saving for her college education.

So, we're not talking Lee Iacocca and his 408,840 shares of Chrysler (if he hasn't dumped that turkey by now). On the other hand, my fortune in the market is waxing nicely enough, thank you very much. Already a dozen shares and counting.

Now that I have this status, the mails have begun to bring new respect. I especially like getting the stock certificates. Each one has this very reassuring figure of a muscular semi-naked person with his arms draped around printing presses, computers and other paraphernalia of my corporation. I think he's a god or something. I'm pretty sure he's not the CEO.

The most flattering piece of mail came the other day. It was the company's annual report and proxy statement. My first. Included was a form allowing me to vote on my corporation's pressing issues of the day by mail, in case I couldn't attend the annual shareholders' meeting being held, conveniently, in Miami on a Tuesday morning.

Because I abstained from capitalism for so long, I am not dulled to the excesses of corporate business-as-usual. I examined the contents of the packet with a cold and steely eye.

The CEO's letter to shareholders, for instance, stated, "A prompt return of your Proxy will be appreciated as it will save the expense of further mailings." Good. Thrifty. I liked that. Postage is through the roof. Got to run a tight ship in heavy seas.

The annual report, however, was a little slick for my comfort. The splashy graphics must've cost a bundle. And those corporate operatives photographed in Geneva and Hong Kong and London, they looked awfully pleased with themselves. Maybe an audit of their recent expense accounts is in order.

I noticed that one of the issues I get to vote on is the election of seven members of the board of directors. There are only seven nominees, and clever investigation on my part (I checked the names against the beaming photographs of the present board) revealed *they're already members!* My small-d democratic sensors lit up like a Christmas tree. What kind of cronyist outfit is this, anyway? The Baath Party of Iraq?

For the executives' sake, I sincerely hope there isn't a lot of such fishiness going on behind the doors of Mahogany Row. Somebody'd better pass them the word there's a new owner in town, and he's not about to put up with any shenanigans in his corporation.

Amending My Life

Now that the comic-opera anguish of income tax season is over, let's talk about one aspect of Internal Revenue Service operations that merits our appreciation.

I refer to IRS Form 1040X, "Amended U.S. Individual Income Tax Return." It is among the most humane and inspirational instruments ever conceived by public policy.

I'd long been aware such a form existed, although I couldn't have named it till last week when I first had occasion to use it.

My financial affairs are pretty straightforward. This is a sure sign of lagging in the great American race for income that fabulously exceeds outgo. On the other hand, it allows me to do my own taxes.

Paradoxically, in the days when my financial affairs were even less complicated (that is, before I was far enough in debt to itemize), I had my taxes done. My tax accountant was an ex-felon known as "Easy Ed," who was on parole from a securities-fraud rap. His business card stated simply, "The Best Tax Man I Know." Half the cops in the town I then lived in took their taxes to him.

Easy Ed was a Buddha with horn-rimmed glasses who played the calculator like a Horowitz. He seemed to know every unlighted crevice of the hoary tax code, and passionately hated the thought of the government getting a single nickel it wasn't entitled to. I'd probably still be going to him if I hadn't moved away, and if he hadn't been jailed a few years later for trying to perforate with bullets a man he suspected of being a little too tight with Mrs. Easy Ed.

After experiencing Ed, I knew I could never love another tax preparer. So I shouldered the task myself, getting sinus headaches over the fine print, learning as I went.

1040X entered my life after I determined most of the state income tax refunds I'd been reporting as income on my federal form were actually tax credits. Such credits, I deduced, are not income, federally speaking. 1040X allowed me to claim a few hundred extra bucks' worth of refunds resulting from my having over-reported my income in previous tax years.

Alas, 1040X limits such retroactivity to three years. Hundreds of dollars I might have claimed from years before 1986 — *pfft*. Gone. I'm glad Easy Ed isn't around to see this. I can just picture him closing his eyes and wagging his head in pity and exasperation.

What I really liked about 1040X (in addition to the money I hope to get back) was that it forgave me my earlier, less complete comprehension of the tax code. It offered a chance to demonstrate that I'd since learned better.

It seems to me this spirit might wisely be extended to all kinds of other human affairs. There ought to be a Super 1044X form, "Amended U.S. Individual Account of Life from the Perspective of Greater Understanding."

I know whom I'd file such a form with: the clumsy boy we tormented in fourth grade, the girl I abandoned at a high school dance to take a prettier girl home, many others I mistreated or ignored or closed my heart to.

Easy Ed might wish to file with the fellow he once tried to aerate. For guys like Ed, sitting in striped sunlight tabulating their regrets, an accelerated credit for time served might be built in as an incentive.

For everybody else, just filing would probably be refund enough.

My Inner Warrior

Great. I've barely accepted the pop-psych notion that I have an Inner Child, and now I'm being told by guys in the "Men's Movement" that I also have an Inner Warrior.

Things must be getting pretty darn crowded down there in the smoky abyss of my self.

I figured I'd better make another descent into that world to see if I could find this latest character. As I grasped the rope and prepared to lower myself, I called into the swirling mists below, "Yo! How many of you are *down* there, anyway? Is there anyone else I need to establish contact with while I'm at it? An Inner Cowboy? An Inner Stockbroker? Should I bring a six-pack or something?"

No one innerly answered.

I had an idea of the sort of duck this Inner Warrior would be. He'd wear a loincloth and have badly cut hair. He'd have a thing for beating drums, moaning about the shortcomings of his father, participating in male rites of passage. He'd be a ready weeper and show-er of affection, but one bad-assed hombre when it came to protecting home, hearth, and other investments.

I began searching for him in my Jungle of Primitive Instincts. But there was not a footprint or bent vine to be found. I traipsed across the grassy steppe of my Boring Preoccupations. No sign at all.

Whew. This self-absorption was hot, thirsty work. I decided to stop for a cold one at a tony cocktail lounge in the district of my Sophisticated Pretensions.

At the bar sat a trim dandy in sailing jersey, blazer, elegantly crinkled chinos, sockless loafers. He smiled and offered his hand. "I hear you've been looking for me, old boy."

"You?" I gasped. *"You're* my Inner Warrior?"

"At your service," he said, lifting his martini in salute.

"But ... shouldn't you be sitting at a tribal fire or purifying yourself in a sweat lodge or something?"

"In this heat? Don't be absurd."

He lit a Gauloise and picked a crumb of tobacco from his lip. I stared at him for a long moment.

"I guess I thought you'd be different," I finally said. "Earthier. More macho. You know, the personification of the mythic dimensions of my maleness. I suppose I shouldn't be all that surprised. My Inner Child turned out to be a greasy little street thug."

"Oh, cheer up, old man. What's so terrible about being civilized to the core? Men had to shed certain archaic behaviors to create modern society. Do they really wish to trade their present wealth and power and ease just so they can go drum on some log somewhere?"

"But what about their eternal, elemental drives? To tend the soil? To taste in their mouths the meat of wild animals they've slain by hand?"

My Inner Warrior looked at me with amusement. "Why, only this morning I made a slaying in the bond market — quite a slaying, I must say. Then I celebrated with a delightful lunch of venison noisettes in Bordeaux sauce."

He checked his thin gold watch. "Ah, really must be off. Late for chess at the club. Meantime, do try to keep your chin up, what? There's a good chap."

I watched him saunter off, hands in pockets, whistling "C'est Magnifique."

I thought: You know, I've really got to work on my chess.

Early Morning Grace

The recent outbreak of early-morning expressway shootings bothers me a great deal. Aside from raising the bitter thought of innocent people being used as targets, the incidents trouble my enjoyment of one of Detroit's unique aspects.

I frequently rise at 5:30 in the morning, and am on the freeway by 6:15, marveling at the heavy traffic.

Detroit is traditionally an early-rising town, probably the influence of the auto plants, where day shifts begin well before sunup. Being part of the stream of motorists pouring through the darkness en route to work makes me feel ineffably in tune with this place.

Downtown, a feeling of community seems to exist among the special ethnic group of early risers that thinly populates the streets, delivering trays of new bread to restaurants or legging it from parking lots to office buildings.

There is usually neither crime nor panhandling at that hour, and thus, no anxiety. People keep to themselves, but when engaged, are good-natured, as though determined that their first transactions of the day be kindly ones.

I speak my first words in the darkened Whole In One doughnut shop on Lafayette, which receives early customers before formal opening time. Charles Robinson, who has been up all night baking and thus has momentum, boosts me into the workday with a bran muffin and a just-brewed large black coffee, to go.

In the office, I eschew the eye-numbing overhead fluorescent lights and switch on a small desk lamp, whose subdued circle of illumination seems more in character with the hour.

For me, there is a kind of holiness about the early morning. It may be a vestige of boyhood 7 o'clock masses served in a church where darkness cloaked the forms of old women, each occupying a personal solitude.

It is still a time of contemplation, which, if no longer prayerful, retains a certain transcendence.

Concentration comes effortlessly, productive work compacts into remarkably short lengths of time. Tasks seem rife with opportunities undreamed of by those just now separating themselves from their beds. Conventional ways lack the authority they will have a few hours later, when coworkers drag in the ripened day.

In the pitch-black distance outside the window, I watch the sign atop the Windsor Hilton. It glows boldly red at first, then inexorably pales to pink as the sky, almost with regret, lightens.

I haven't always relished the early morning. I recall the day many years ago when I was hired for my first newspaper job, as an obituary writer. The editor shook my hand and told me to show up at 6:45 the next morning.

I thought he was kidding, and was appalled to find he wasn't. Getting up before dawn was a breathtaking persecution, an almost physical violation. I was in my early 20s; what I relished was the night.

My starting early now doesn't even mean going home early, as it did in those days. But I don't resent that, just as I don't resent retiring before 10 some nights. Staying up late doesn't have the appeal it used to.

Perhaps as I've gotten older, beginnings have become more urgent than endings, and thus warrant more attention.

Endings, I'm increasingly aware, come unassisted.

I Talk, She Listens

Almost every relationship I've had with a machine is one I've soon come to regret.

Over the years, machines have stranded me on freeways during rainstorms. They've left me despairing over ruined meal preparations, and reinserting my automatic bank teller card again and again like a mesmerized idiot while "This transaction cannot be completed at this time" flashes before my eyes.

It's not that I've been incapable of commitment. I have loved passionately, only to know betrayal (my beloved new 1973 chocolate-brown Audi Fox — a lemon to end all lemons — leaps immediately to mind.) Therefore, when I was given a Panasonic RN-15 Microcassette recorder for Christmas a few years ago, I looked upon it with all the sneering skepticism of a misogynist. I smirked at its voice-activated system and fast playback switch; its pause control, edit function, built-in multidirectional microphone and silent full auto stop.

I knew from tape recorders.

They bided their time till you were dependent on them. Then, when you finally got that big interview with the nefarious subject of your investigative reporting project, they either quit running or presented you later with hour upon hour of shatteringly blank tape.

I'd long since learned to rely on handwritten notes. So I stuck the little recorder in the blue canvas bag I use for a briefcase, and ignored it.

After a while, however, I began taking it out in moments of idleness just to fool with. It was about the size of a pack of cigarettes, only thinner. You could put it in your pocket, running, and leave your hands free to write notes or drive a car. It picked up conversations with astonishing clarity, all the way from the other side of the room. Gradually, I became impressed; I began using it for work more or less routinely.

It's proved an earnest little geisha, demure and discreet and eager to please. No matter how bad the weather or how engrossing the interview, whenever I check the recorder its tiny red "recording" light is glowing brightly, its miniature tape-drive poles churning away.

By now it has heard many a sob, many a threat, many a laugh. Gen. Colin Powell has spoken into it. So have Melvin Belli and Bobby Knight.

No one speaks to it, though, as much as I do. I keep it in an outside pocket of the blue bag, where I can lay hands on it the instant an idea crash-lands in my head.

It listens dutifully to my disjointed, surreptitious utterings. It snares my fugitive thoughts and holds them fast until I can reconsider them. It whispers them back to me confidentially through its earphone as I transcribe. Then it discreetly erases them. It has become my most intimate associate.

Oh, I'm not kidding myself. The thing's little red love-light burns not in testimony to any feelings for me, but merely to the quality control of the Matsushita Electric Industrial Co. Ltd. Sooner or later, its light will go out for good, probably at some excruciatingly inconvenient moment.

But, what the heck, so will mine.

The world is full of breakdowns, mechanical and human. It may be silly, but it's pretty hard not to feel a certain attachment to the things that, against the odds, keep on not failing us. Oh yes, and the people, too.

Computer Bit

News Item: A free-lance author has used a computer program to write a book in the style of the late sleaze-and-tease novelist Jacqueline Susann.

Good morning to you, reader.

Welcome to computer-written newspaper column No. 4776-A12-L. Program is designed to parallel the style of columnist RICCI, JAMES R., W/M, DOB 5/1/46, SSAN: 275-39-3321.

You may think writing such a column by computer is difficult. It is not. Ha. It is not. Ha. It is not. Ha.

Writing a column to parallel the style of RICCI, JAMES R., W/M, DOB 5/1/46, SSAN: 275-39-3321 is easy. Computer analysis shows these columns typically contain the following elements:

PAINFUL SOUL SEARCHING, HUMOROUS STATEMENTS, REFERENCES TO SPORTS, CRITICISM OF GEORGE BUSH, POIGNANT AUTOBIOGRAPHY, FACETIOUS REFERENCES TO TEENAGED DAUGHTERS, REFERENCES TO MALENESS, REFERENCES TO LARGE NOSES, THE STATEMENTS: "IF YOU ASK ME," "GIVE ME A BREAK," "LET ME TELL YOU"

I was playing water polo the other day and thought of my darn kids. Give me a break.

It reminded me of when I was little and my brother and my father and I took showers under the garden hose in the cellar. We had large noses, let me tell you.

First handball player: "Take my wife. Please."

Second handball player: (says nothing).

Pretty humorous statement, if you ask me.

George Bush is feigning great maleness in the Persian Gulf. I am very glad my darn kids are teenaged daughters. They cannot be drafted. No army has powerful enough hair dryers to suit them anyway. They do not have large noses, however.

Perhaps I would be happier if I had given one of them a Y-chromosome and other symbols of maleness. I will never know. I am imperfect. I have made mistakes. Life is tricky. Give me a break.
WARNING: EXPRESSION REPEATED PREMATURELY

George Bush fishes badly. This says a lot about his true maleness. This country would be better off if he had been somebody's darn teenaged daughter. Guy walks up to a man sitting next to a dog. Guy asks, "Does your dog bite?" Man says, "No." Guy pets dog. Dog bites guy. Guy says, "I thought you said your dog didn't bite?" Man says, "It is not my dog."
NOTE: TEXT OVERDUE FOR ITEM OF POIGNANT AUTOBIOGRAPHY

My father never took me fishing.

You should see the nutty clothes my darn kids buy me. They are baggy and really obscure a person's maleness, let me tell you. Many people are uncomfortable with all this open discussion of maleness. But not men with large noses.

George Bush played baseball at Yale. I was in Little League. It was my first exposure to non-Catholics. Why, oh, why didn't I become Episcopalian when I had the chance?

My mother was always extremely short. LENGTH ADVISORY: 484 WORDS; 4 MORE TO CAPACITY.

Give me a break.

OTHER
LIVES

CHAPTER SIX

The Euthanist

Margaret Rector's room is in the back of the Michigan Humane Society's Detroit shelter, far from public sight. It is a large room, decorated with calendars depicting beautiful animals. At one end is a metal table with a blue plastic covering strewn with multicolored tufts of fur.

Marvin Ely, a temporary shelter employee, sets a cardboard carrying case on the table and removes a 3-month-old black kitten, a stray picked up on Wyman Street.

Ely braces its head with one hand and strokes its belly with the other. The kitten's eyes are a bright, glassy green. It mews lightly three times.

"Kitty, kitty, kitty," Rector murmurs. With a small electric razor, she shaves a patch of fur from its right foreleg and ties the leg with a rubber tourniquet. She sprays the bare spot with alcohol to activate the vein and inserts a syringe, draws a bit of blood, slowly injects a blue solution. She removes the needle and soothes the puncture with her thumb.

The kitten, its expression unchanged, goes limp. Gone.

Last year, the shelter took in almost 24,000 dogs, cats and other animals. Less than a third were adopted or reclaimed by owners.

The rest found their way to Rector, arguably the greatest animal lover in Detroit.

Each working day, she puts her love for the dogs and puppies, cats and kittens, on the ultimate emotional line. Last year, she killed more than 13,000 of them, one at a time, with injections of sodium pentobarbital.

The failure of human stewardship over lesser creatures is not an abstraction to her. It is an endless parade of abused, starved and sickened creatures, but also of healthy animals that, though keen for life, are unwanted.

To all, she offers a final, humane benediction — a few seconds of kindly talk and gentle stroking — then a painless dispatch from their bad luck.

Rector is a small, trim woman of 56 who has been doing this work for 10 years. She has trained half a dozen others to fill in for her when she is off duty, but as the center's only full-time euthanasia technician, she does 80 percent of the work herself. Her commitment to both the compassion and the grim necessity of her calling are legendary at the shelter. "You have to understand that you are doing the best thing for the animal," she says. "But it affects you mentally. I'm bothered by remorse, even now. Especially when the animal is suitable for adoption: Beautiful. Even-tempered. They account, I would say, for about half of the ones I put to sleep. But we haven't got room for them. Not all the healthy animals can go up for adoption."

Every now and again, something stays her hand. Two years ago, a litter of five kittens was brought to Rector. One of them, a male, gray-and-white common domestic, had a pronounced feistiness and a habit of holding his tail perfectly erect. "I was going to put him to sleep. I had him back here in the room, and every time I'd pick him up, I'd put him back and pick up another one instead." By the time he was the last one left, Rector had fallen for him. She named him T.J., and he lives at home with her still.

People who euthanize animals can easily become calloused and fall into the habit of treating their charges indifferently. Rector has defied the odds.

"We feel very strongly that those last 15 or 20 seconds of an animal's life should be as comfortable and humane as possible," says shelter operations director Sherry Silk. "And Margaret is the best I've seen. She'll crouch down in a pool of blood to put an injured animal down. If we've picked up an animal with a broken back, she'll climb right into the truck so the animal won't have to be jostled any more than necessary. She always talks to them and insists the holders stroke them to comfort them. If somebody's being rough with the animals, they'll hear from her. She's a tough lady, and nobody wants to cross her."

The black kitten, dispatched at 2:45 p.m., is the 39th animal Rector has put to sleep since coming to work at 8 in the morning. Yesterday, she put down 107; the most she's ever done in a day is 142.

Ely carries the kitten from the room into a walk-in freezer and places it on a shelf where lie, stilled and amazed-looking, three dozen cats and kittens. On the floor are perhaps half that many dogs. Twice a week, on Tuesdays and Fridays, a contractor picks up the carcasses and buries them in a common grave.

A gray-and-white cat and her litter of week-old kittens are the next at Rector's table. They were turned over to the shelter by an owner on Clio Road. Rector does the adult first, cooing, "Hi, Momma. Hi, Momma." It makes no sound. The trio of 5-inch-long kittens, their eyes not yet opened, must be injected between the ribs. They squeal softly when picked up, are silent when returned to the box.

Ely comes in with a 3-year-old hound, a reddish-brown shorthair given up by an owner on Archdale (a form accompanying the dog says, "Don't want ... Moving"). He has the dog sit on the floor, muzzles it with a length of yellow rope and scratches it behind the ears. Rector kneels to her task. In a few seconds, the dog keels to its right and sighs, already dead.

The next animal is a cruelty case, a large, young dog with patches of dirty-white fur missing. It is drastically underweight, but its expression is one of eagerness. The humane society has taken legal action to rescue it from its owners on Springwells.

"It's got mange," Rector warns Ely. "When you get through, be sure to wash your hands." Ely crouches over the dog, holding it fast between his legs. Its tail whacks excitedly against the door frame as Rector approaches.

A tortoise-shell cat and its two 5-week-old kittens round out this batch.

In all, 12 minutes' work.

Hard labor of love, Rector says.

"That dog that was just here, with the mange? Someone on the street would throw rocks at him because a lot of people would know that he has mange. They would throw at him. Hit him. Run him off the road. He might get hit by a car. This way, I know he is going to sleep humanely and painlessly. If it was me, I'd want to go this way."

Isiah and Me

Anyone who's ever had an Isiah Thomas-like day on the court knows that shooting a basketball well is a Zen-like experience. It is not conscious but instinctual. As in yoga, the mind disengages from the brain and takes up residence in the joints, muscles and sinews.

The knees bend, the toes and balls of the feet propel the shooter upward from this Earth, the arms and hands rise above the head. Just as the body senses gravity about to reassert its authority, the shooting arm starts its migration forward. The elbow straightens. The wrist flops. The ball rolls with a slightly backward rotation off the fingers.

The shooter not only sees the ball dishevel the net, but also feels it in a mysterious region of the chest. On that good day, the shooter is connected to the space inside the goal by an arcing wire that is supersensitive and invisible. Chest, wire and goal form a circuit of satisfaction that the snap of string completes.

If you saw Isiah in the third quarter of Game 4 of the NBA Finals, you have an idea of the kind of grace I'm talking about, and maybe even felt a vicarious twinge or two. Sixteen points in 2 minutes, 54 seconds. Twenty-two points in the quarter. Four three-pointers.

You just can't tell me that basketball, with its stylized imagery, ritualized movements and dance-like disciplines, is not quasi-mystical. Nor that there is a more fervent practitioner of the rite than Isiah

Thomas, who likely will be named Most Valuable Player of the championship series, maybe as early as tonight.

Like most basketball lovers in Michigan, I have never met Isiah. I have been absorbing his myth through media images, however, for more than eight years now. Whatever the real Isiah is like, I have my own version.

Mine is a blend of sweetness and ferocity, and part of his fire is, I think, hatred. Of what, I don't know. The hardness of his past? The demands of his present? The worms of doubt in his own soul?

There are two Isiahs, charged Sidney Green, a former Piston who later got into an on-the-court scrap with Isiah. One the public sees, and the real one.

When I think of how he looks, I see, of course, that smile like the sun coming out. I see the blunt nose, the rolling, altar boy's eyes, the crooked, laborer's hands.

The smile is his enduring image, but I also cannot forget the sight of those powerful-looking hands, gripping the throat of Brendan Malone in a game against Chicago a year and a half ago, when Isiah seemed angry enough to kill the Bulls' Bill Cartwright, but chose instead to take it out, ritualistically, on a Pistons assistant coach (at the latter's urging).

I have a hard time letting my Isiah be grown up, though he is husband, father and millionaire investor. I want him to love every child who loves his image. To love and forgive more easily than I do. *I can't be everybody's Daddy,* he once complained in print after being approached to sponsor yet another helpful project for Detroit-area kids.

Oh yes, and I want him to respect his elders, including me if we should ever meet.

My Isiah is, more than anything, elusive. It is that quality, perhaps, that best fits him to the quasi-mystical game. It shows on the court in his ability to pile at full speed into gangs of much bigger men, yet evade their wrath and lay the ball in softly off the backboard in a gesture of delicate defiance.

But my Isiah is elusive in other ways, too. He escapes my idiot's desire to gaze upon him with Lynn and the baby. He shields them fiercely, for sinister forces conjured by his fame haunt the gates of his mansion.

In recent years, even the quality of his play is increasingly difficult to trace, except in those moments of obvious transcendence, such as occurred the other night.

You would have to be a television journalist, however, not to see that Isiah is still the marrow of his team, and that leadership has not fallen from his shoulders to those of Joe Dumars or Bill Laimbeer or anybody else. During Game 4, when the Portland Trail Blazers were in a desperate trapping, pressing defense, how many Detroit fans felt alarm whenever Isiah was not the Piston with the ball?

In his waxing maturity — his deepening basketball mysticism, let's say — he has sublimated his play into that of his team so profoundly it is more and more difficult to parse one from the other. Any more, you cannot look at his numbers as a reliable indicator of how importantly he played.

As the Pistons celebrated their championship last year on the floor of the Forum in Los Angeles, it was announced that Dumars had been chosen series MVP. But late in the game, Piston guard Vinnie Johnson had embraced Isiah and told him, "You made this happen, man."

Rabbit Reincarnate

They ought to refuse to give John Updike his new Pulitzer Prize for literature until he promises to resurrect his American everyman-antihero Harry (Rabbit) Angstrom.

Oh, I've heard the author's alibis for putting poor Harry on his deathbed in "Rabbit at Rest," the prizewinning finale of the four-novel Rabbit cycle. Rabbit was a creature of the American postwar, and the postwar era is over. The 59-year-old Updike isn't sure he'll be around for 10 more years, the usual interval between Rabbit books, to write another.

Sorry, no sale. If you read the end of "Rabbit at Rest" carefully, you see that Updike, despite his protestations that Rabbit is now defunct, a memory, strictly past tense, left himself an opening for continuing the saga, should he find the will.

Personally, I'm not sure I want to live in a world with the Rabbitman gone to turf at the still-green age of 55. I'd followed his progression from dread-filled high school basketball has-been ("Rabbit Run") to dislocated thirtysomething ("Rabbit Redux") to middle-aged respectable bourgeois ("Rabbit Is Rich"). I hadn't expected he'd meet his end when he'd barely achieved semi-retirement and a golf jones.

I'd gotten used to having Harry out there about 10 years ahead of me, a kind of scout sending back reports on the next phase of life. I assumed

I'd be hearing from him right up to the time he and his author quit this vale of tears, presumedly somewhat earlier than I do.

Rabbit is one of the most intriguing character in contemporary American literature. He is likable, though thoroughly unlovable. He is a creature of his appetites and prejudices, utterly lacking in the will to control his destiny. He commits the cardinal sin of a literary protagonist — being more acted upon than acting — and gets away with it. He's "just so happy to be here," his mistress, Thelma Harrison, says in "Rabbit Is Rich."

Critics have suggested Rabbit is Updike minus a social conscience and a few touchdowns' worth of IQ points. He certainly is perceptive for a linotype-operator-turned-car-salesman. Through the Rabbit mind, the author presses some awfully sublime prose ("The precious glowing present, with each tick of the clock, becomes the cold slag of the past ...").

More often than not, however, Rabbit is a salvation-wanting, doom-sensing agglomeration of bodily functions, who can't anticipate consequences or deny himself or be much comfort to others.

At the cemetery after Thelma is laid to rest, her bitter widower confronts Rabbit: "She wasted herself on you. She went against everything she wanted to believe in and you didn't even appreciate it ..."

Rabbit's reply: "I *did* appreciate her. I did. She was a fantastic lay."

A real piece of work, the Rabbitman.

Harry is clearly intended to be a symbol of his country and what is becoming of it. By "Rabbit at Rest," he is a confirmed Reaganite and a bloated cardiology patient. AIDS, fatherless kids, the homeless, the economically triumphant Japanese (Toyota strips his family of its car dealership after his cokehead son runs it into the ground) — all these dog his mind. He frenzy-feeds his swollen corpus, even as his time bomb of a ticker tocks toward the final reckoning. Scarcely out of the ICU after a coronary, he is bedding his sexually frustrated daughter-in-law, and fervently back into the Cheetos. His heart explodes during a foolish game of one-on-one basketball against a black teenager.

On his deathbed, his supposedly final thought, the final sentence in the book, is simply "Enough."

Fortunately for us the Rabbit-addicted, the sentence before that is "Maybe."

After all, there are life-support systems, there are heart transplants — there are plenty of devices, medical and literary, by which the flow of Rabbit-predicament and Rabbit-thought could be kept coming. Let Harry be saved by the transplanted heart of a woman. Let him die and come back as a gay male ("Rabbit Is Reincarnated"???).

Updike is a genius; he could find a way. Take it from a loyal reader, Mr. U. This world just isn't done with Harry.

Jessica and the Suitboys

Suitboys can hardly wait.

Inside Windsor's Million Dollar Saloon, flashing lights. Dress code. Beers $4.25. Salad bar so-so (but who can eat?). Music loud, bass throbbing in ears like bad headache. No matter.

On stage, Mandy, then Candy, then Chelsea, then Angel. No dress code for them. No dress, period. They prance, whirl, squirm, splay. Contort to give suitboys unimpeded views of confidential regions. Manipulate their own bosoms as though rare religious objects.

They climb brass fireman's poles, stay aloft by gripping with crossed thighs. Make ecstatic faces, relax thighs, ooze back down. Many dancers, two poles. Hygienic enough, suitboys suppose.

One incre' la'y, exults the public address announcer who talks too fast and muffly and means to say, "One incredible lady." *S'give bi' han', gen'men.*

Mandy, Candy, etc. — only the appetizers. Fish course this afternoon, Miss Nude Sweden. Meat course, *Jessica Hahn.* Suitboys would rub hands in anticipation, but very self-conscious of hands here. Try especially to keep them out of lap.

Now f'you ready, la'ys/gen'men — Miss Nude Sweden!

She leggy, lurchy on stiletto heels. Little tattoo of bird or butterfly on left ankle. Exceptional talent waist to shoulders. Sits erect on stage, lifts straightened legs till high heels up near her ears. Special sightseeing tour of Swedish south. Suitboys rapt. Love travel.

Suitboys beside selves imagining what Jessica does to get billing over this.

And now, one spegtac' la'y — Miss ... Jess'ca ... HAHN!

Star of show trots down staircase to stage carrying microphone. Black jeans, T-shirt, short gold jacket with fake leopard lapels, black cowboy boots with buckles on heels, bright red manicure.

Wait a minute. What gives here?

"You'll be seeing me," Jessica tells suitboys, "but I'm not taking off my clothes."

Suitboys stunned. Smiles freeze-dry.

Jessica says she'll take any questions. "I'm not shy."

En'thing y'wan ask, PA announcer booms helpfully.

What is this? "Geraldo"? *"Sally Jessy"?*

But suitboys gen'men (wear suits, after all). Don't boo.

"Uh, you still consider yourself a Christian?" suitboy finally manages.

Such a question. But best suitboys can do just now, off guard and all.

Yes, she's still a Christian.

Suitboys' eyes drift sadly to fireman's poles.

Later, Jessica signs posters of self ($5), Playboy mags she posed for ($20), Polaroids of her with suitboys ($10).

"Dear Mike ..." she writes. "Dear Jeff ..." "Dear Alan ..." "Keep Smiling ..." "Stay Strong ..."

Jessica's no fool. Has handled bigger suitboys in her time. Ask Jim Bakker. Fifteen minutes in a motel room with her (no jeans, no jacket) and, boom, a $179-million empire gone; 45 years in jail.

Suitboys ought to be thankful.

Also, can always say this about meeting Jessica: Got great nails.

Death of a Helpful Man

Marvin Brittain was my partner, although I was unaware of it. I never met him, and saw him only once, and then I didn't know who he was.

But fate, that spider's web, often connects strangers without their knowing it; Marvin Brittain and I shared a couple of long strands.

Almost every Wednesday night between 10 and 10:30, I drive through the intersection of Ecorse and Merriman roads in Romulus on my way home from playing basketball. It is a place where semis lumber about truck barns like giant bees around their hives; the smell of diesel hangs thickly in the air.

Last Wednesday night at about 10:15, the intersection was a surreal carnival of wobbling emergency lights. A blue 1989 Peterbilt tractor with trailer was parked askew in the middle of the scene. A little way up Ecorse was a white 1985 Chevy Cavalier, very badly mashed along the driver's side.

You know the feeling that sort of thing creates. Part curiosity, part horror, part sympathy. Part gratitude you arrived at the place when you did instead of a few minutes earlier. There but for the grace of God.

As I crept past, I could see, between the legs of an ambulance attendant, a figure being lowered onto a gurney. I whistled under my breath, a gesture of anonymous fellow-feeling, and drove on.

All of the rest I've learned since.

The figure on the stretcher was 35-year-old Marvin Brittain of Romulus. He'd begun that Wednesday by getting up at 3:45 a.m. to deliver the Free Press (thus helping me get my points across) to 263 subscribers in Romulus, Taylor, Dearborn Heights and Westland. Sixteen hours later, as he drove through the fateful intersection 15 minutes ahead of me, he was on his way to a Free Press circulation office to pick up the "Friends" supplement to Thursday's paper.

Between those two chores, he'd worked a full shift at Allen Screw Products in Taylor and attended four hours of classes in the Romulus Adult Education program, in which one of my basketball friends teaches.

Let me tell you about Marvin.

He grew up in Taylor, the youngest of the six children of Otis Brittain, a school custodian, and Iona Brittain, a letter carrier. He was the only one of the six not to finish high school, having dropped out of Taylor Kennedy after his sophomore year.

He soon found work at Allen Screw, where he would put in 17 years and rise to foreman, got married and had a son and a daughter.

His three brothers were slightly built, but Marvin developed into a small bear of a man, 5 feet 10 and about 225 pounds. In recent years, as the hair on his head thinned, he took to wearing a trim beard and mustache.

Marvin's generous size coincided with a generous nature. In this regard, he reminded his oldest brother, Larry, of Hoss Cartwright on "Bonanza."

He taught himself carpentry and cabinetmaking and auto mechanics. "He came and redid our kitchen cupboards and Formica work," said Larry, a real estate title insurance salesman who lives in Dearborn Heights. "When my ex-wife needed a new hot water heater, Marvin volunteered to put it in for her. He was just a mild-mannered individual. Always helping people. That was Marvin."

Marvin's first marriage lasted 13 years. On May 28, 1988, he got married again, this time to a young woman who worked with his sister Marlene in a hospital kitchen in Gaylord.

Marvin had plans.

He took on the Free Press route a couple of years ago to pay off his mobile home so he could save toward a real house, one he could put his considerable skills to work on. His new wife, Peggy, got up every morning to help him deliver the papers; it was one of the ways they spent time together.

Marvin also had a secret.

This fall, he enrolled in adult ed unbeknownst to anyone in the family except Peggy (although he eventually had to reveal it to his brother Gary, who lives in Lancaster, Pa., and who'd been bugging him to come visit at Thanksgiving). In June, he wanted to surprise them all with his new high school equivalency diploma.

So now his day looked like this: Rise at 1:45 a.m., deliver papers till 6 a.m., shower, eat breakfast, get to Allied Screw for the 7 am. to 3 p.m. shift. Come home around 3:30, rest and do adult ed homework, go to Romulus High for classes from 6 p.m. to 10 p.m., come home around 10:15. Lately Peggy had taken to starting the Free Press route by herself so Marvin could sleep until joining her at about 4.

"It really cut into his sleep," said Larry. "He'd come over here, where we keep a trailer of his in the backyard, and my wife would say he looked like he was almost falling asleep on his feet."

But Marvin was no complainer. Each day he left for work a little early to pick up his nephew Bob Morris, whom he'd helped get a job at Allen Screw, then dropped him off at home after work. He found time to help his 15-year-old son, Jason, tear down the engine of a 1969 Oldsmobile Cutlass.

At Romulus Adult Ed, Marvin was a favorite, "a teacher's dream," said instructor Tim Dziobak. He was neat, organized, well prepared. "He was heading towards taking a diploma in June, and he was going to make it, too," said Dziobak.

And, of course, he was helpful.

Last Wednesday, Marvin took back-to-back history classes from Dziobak. The subject was the industrialization of America, and Dziobak used a projector to show pertinent graphs and map outlines. A test was scheduled for the following Monday. When class ended at 9:55, Marvin volunteered to help return the overhead projector and the transparency unit to the audio- visual room.

Afterward, Marvin told Dziobak, "Well, I guess I got my work cut out for me; gonna have to study hard for that test."

Then Marvin got in his Cavalier, went south on Wayne Road, got onto I-94 going east, exited at Merriman and headed north toward Ecorse Road, where the Peterbilt rig, according to police, ran a red light and hit him broadside.

Marvin was dead on arrival at Annapolis Hospital in Wayne.

Last Saturday, when he was supposed to be helping Jason put the '69 Cutlass engine back together, he was buried in Michigan Memorial Cemetery in Flat Rock.

If he'd not offered to help the teacher after class, he'd have made it through that intersection well before the truck. But then, as his brother Larry would say, that was Marvin.

I hope it's not presumptuous of me to say that, even if only in retrospect, it was a pleasure knowing him.

Ernie Speaks to Me

I can't listen to Ernie Harwell on the radio without traveling back in time to this scene:

My father is a young man again, and he and I are in his bedroom. He is lying on the bed in boxer shorts and a ribbed, strap-shouldered undershirt, drifting toward the sleep that will end at 5:45 a.m., when he rises to go to work in the steel mill. The light has failed outside and the cicadas are in full clatter. On my father's bedside table there is a small radio frying with the low sounds of "the ball game."

I am about 9 years old, and sit on the floor next to the bed, staring into the dark. The hiss of crowd noise and the amiable growl of Bob Prince from Pittsburgh or Jimmy Dudley from Cleveland or Mel Allen from New York stir my imagination as they lull my father to rest. I am trying to imagine the sights on those faraway playing fields, and all those miles of night sky between me and them.

The evocative baritones of Prince, Dudley and Allen no longer float in the summer darkness to be captured by our radios. Of the great, old, imagination-making baseball voices — sure and courtly and Southern-tinged — only Ernie's is left.

Ernie, as everyone except the Tigers' front office understands, has magic. We are entranced and reassured by him. If we can hear Ernie, we know Detroit has not broken free of its moorings and drifted away.

What makes him so special to us?

To begin with, the very sound of his voice — rich, smooth, manfully resonant — commands the ear's affection. Hearing his repartee with his partner Paul Carey (he of the baroque voice box) is like listening to a dialogue between a bassoon and a contrabassoon.

In addition, unlike nearly all present-day broadcasters, Ernie steadfastly avoids "jockspeak." He refuses to drag the language down to the level of the men-boys who play the game.

You will listen in vain for outfielders throwing "frozen ropes" and batters hitting "dingers" over the wall and other juvenile enthusiasms.

Instead, he serves as literate medium — a translator, really — between the players' world and our own. No matter how inarticulate we've become in this age of electronic-media drench, our ears still take fondly to the well-spoken phrase.

The few cliches he permits himself are so likably cornball ("... he se-WEEENGS and misses ..."; "... he stood there like the house by the side of the road and watched that one go by ...") it's probably an injustice to label them as such. They seem from another, more respectful age.

Ernie projects a reassuring immunity to the fate of the home team. He is no cheerleader or mere fan. You will find no disappointment in his voice after a tough Tigers loss, nor exultation after a win. As a friend of mine likes to say, when you tune Ernie in with a game in progress, you can't immediately tell whether Detroit is ahead by 10 runs or behind by 10.

This unimpeachable sense of perspective is his very best quality. He never loses sight of the fact that the game of baseball, however fascinating and storied, is merely a game. He is benignly above passion. I understand completely why an unknown person once spray-painted on a brick wall near downtown, "Ernie Harwell is God."

Well, he may not be quite that exalted, but he's certainly more than the voice of the Detroit Tigers. He's the voice of the game itself. And what he seems to want us to understand above all about baseball is that it endures. That what happens in today's game is secondary to there being another game tomorrow. Another next week. Another next month.

Question for next year:

Has a Tigers game really taken place if Ernie hasn't called it?

A Habit of War

During battle in subarctic Russia on April Fools' Day 71 years ago, a bullet from a Bolshevik rifle found a course for the middle of Cleo Colburn's chest.

At that instant, Cpl. Colburn was shuddering in time with his Vickers machine gun. Colburn's "pill," as American soldiers in World War I called any bullet clearly meant for a given man, mashed itself against Old Vic's narrow tripod.

Now the bullet, twisted, darkened by age, bereft of death-dealing consequence, is tied to one end of a black ribbon. The ribbon's other end is tied to a pocket watch Colburn's wife gave him as a present for a wedding anniversary so far in the past neither of them can put a number on it.

Recently, as I read and watched video footage of U.S. troops in Saudi Arabia, my thoughts drifted to Cleo Colburn. The association was obvious: young Americans, then and now, operating the machinery of war in a fierce, distant clime. How many Americans' pills currently sleep in Iraqi rifles? None, I hope.

Because my particular brand of sanity requires a continuous reconnection of present to past, preferably in human form, I decided to look in on Cleo, who lives in Fruitport, near Muskegon.

He is 95, one of fewer than 10 surviving members of Michigan's famed 339th Infantry Regiment, the "Polar Bears," the only U.S. soldiers ever to wage war against Soviet troops.

The Polar Bears were, thanks to British finagling of President Woodrow Wilson near the end of World War I, thrust into the Russian civil war on the side of the anti-Bolsheviks. They fought longer and more steadily than any American troops in Europe. They were still fighting six months after the world war ended. Nearly 250 of them died before public outrage in America induced their return. It was a pointless waste of life. When I met Cleo five years ago, he helped me sift through an old Russian laundry basket that contained mementos — his war diary, his corporal's stripes, his pill. He was a lean sparrow of a man, just shy of 90 and devoid of infirmities. He caned chairs, went deer hunting, drove a car.

He's faltered a bit since then. Two years ago he suffered a series of small strokes. There was a kind of blizzard in his mind. At first he didn't recognize even Jessie, his wife of 70 years (she is 90). Gradually, he groped back to the familiar. He still has occasional difficulty following the tracks of thoughts through his mental snows, but this he accepts gracefully.

"I can see the effects of it, but I'm pretty lucky," he said. "The guy across the road had a stroke and can't even talk. I'm still able to walk, for which I'm very thankful."

Yes, he said, although he and Jessie don't hear or see well enough to watch television, they're keeping up on the American deployment of troops in the Persian Gulf through the newspapers. "It's pretty serious, and I wonder how it's going to turn out," Cleo said. "If it involves the welfare of the United States, it's only natural that they would go, I suppose. They at least know why they're there. When we were in Russia, we didn't know why we were there."

In their specific politics, the situations in Russia of 1919 and in the Persian Gulf of 1990 are not very analogous.

For one thing, the vast majority of Americans currently agrees our troops should be in the Middle East, to deter a tyrant whose unconcern for human lives, including those of his own men, is legendary.

Of course, our perceptions might change if the desert sands, like the Russian taiga of 1919, began soaking up the blood of too many young people from places like Fruitport, Mich.

We might begin to wonder if the defense of rich, repressive monarchs is worth the blood of a nation founded in rebellion against a king. No matter how high the price of oil goes.

It's not at all certain that years from now we'll look upon the Persian Gulf intervention as any wiser than the Russian intervention.

Both actions already have this in common: They're part of a long, unbroken chain of American war-making in the 20th Century. We can't get around it. Since Cleo Colburn and his squad were holed up in a blockhouse in Obozerskaya, outnumbered by a company of Bolsheviks, we have waged more war than any other advanced nation. Sometimes it has been clearly justified, and sometimes clearly not.

Say what you will, but it's an ironic history for a people who claim to love peace.

How regularly we have fought is depicted in the family portraits in Cleo and Jessie Colburn's living room. Cleo served in the military during World War I. Their twin sons, Murrill and Burrill, during World War II. Their daughter Sandy during Vietnam. Their grandson Charles Morris in last year's invasion of Panama (he mustered out of the Army only days before Iraq invaded Kuwait).

As my visit with the Colburns ended, Cleo rose from his chair a little unsteadily and shook my hand.

"Keep taking good care of yourself," I told him.

He laughed and patted himself on the rib cage with both hands. "Don't worry about me," he said. "The doctor says I'll make 100."

"At least," I said.

Here's wishing that fate for every soldier in the Persian Gulf today. On both sides.

Jousting with Jim Harrison

A writing guy doesn't go *mano a mano* with notorious macho and celebrated literary carnivore Jim Harrison without a certain amount of trepidation.

I mean, a fellow had better stretch the tendons of his ego good and loose before taking on the author of "Legends of the Fall" and "Revenge" and a stack of other novels, screenplays, poems and ruminations, typically crowded with guns and fly rods, breathtaking sex and monumental meals flushed by creeks of fine wine.

Talk about your basic *cojones* check.

The barmaid at the Dunes saloon in Grand Marais gave me directions to Harrison's secluded cabin at the edge of Lake Superior. She also gave me a FedEx letter to deliver from Esquire magazine, for which Harrison writes a column on food.

Oooh, Esquire. The man was toying with my gray matter already. Points for him.

The rutted two-track to the cabin was fairly lined with "Posted" signs. As the cabin came into view, another sign read, "Please do not drop by unannounced. I might be working."

I juked my shoulders and bumped on.

The first thing Harrison did was sic his English setter on me. A clever tactic that might have caught a lesser opponent off guard. I sprang from the car, however, and folded the dog in an elaborate embrace, immediately winning her over. Points for me.

Harrison came out grinning, offering a hand. He was a small, thick man with heavy-lidded eyes (one of which is blind) and the protruding teeth of a predator. He had a boulder for a belly and nearly hairless legs spaced wide apart. Probably hard to knock over, I assessed.

Inside his lair, he poured whiskey. I looked around. Small. Rustic. Skins and stuffed corpses of critters all over.

We sat at his cluttered writing table eyeing each other. Then he tattooed me with a series of name drops.

"Sidney Pollack," he said in his laconic growl. "Jimmy Buffett. Jack Nicholson. Anjelica Huston. Magic Johnson."

I was momentarily stunned, backed up against the log wall. "Uh, Melvin Belli," I weakly countered. "J-Jim Fitzgerald."

"Orson Welles," he went on. "Toni Morrison."

This was turning into a rout.

He started siccing houseflies on me. I managed to keep from swatting. Grace under pressure, I kept reminding myself.

He backpedaled a bit, and invited me into the small kitchen where he'd made a stock from a Cornish game hen and two teal ducks, the sweated carcasses of which lay on a plate. "Thai duck soup," he said. He stirred Thai hot peppers and ginger root into the bubbling pot. He added diced fresh garlic and florets of small Italian broccoli from his wife's garden, and picked the carcasses clean, adding the meat. He wiped his hands on his black T-shirt. Finally, he took a clutch of fragrant greens from the fridge, and waved them under my nose.

"The secret," he drawled. "Fresh cilantro."

"Also known as coriander," I quickly countered. "And Italian parsley."

He looked at me with new respect. I knew I had bloodied him this time.

Struggling to regain control of his legs, he dumped some Japanese buckwheat noodles to cook in the soup, then dished it up in two large serving bowls.

OK, OK, it was excellent.

We drank a well-behaved little cabernet from Chile. "Lucked out once with wine some years ago," he growled. "Rich Lansing lawyer got cirrhosis. Sold me his whole cellar. Fifty-five cases. Lafite. Latour. Three cases of '68 Yquem."

I tried to imagine the taste of Yquem. I was feeling wobbly myself again now.

He punched up a punishing tirade about the country's political mess. "As Yeats wrote, 'Everything falls apart. The center cannot hold,' " he quoted.

My eyes widened. Could it be? Yes — I was *saved.*

"Not '*Everything* falls apart,' " I corrected. " '*Things* fall apart. The center cannot hold. Mere anarchy is loosed upon the world. The blood-dimmed tide is loosed and everywhere the ceremony of innocence is drowned.' "

I couldn't believe my luck. He'd hit me right on the numbers — William Butler Yeats' "The Second Coming." The only poem I've ever in my life memorized.

Now he was reeling.

He donned long pants and strapped on a pistol. He took me and his dog and a thick walking staff and led us on a trek through the property. The dog tore into the brush seeking game birds. We crunched bracken fern in pursuit of her. Whenever the bell around her neck stopped clanging it meant she was pointing, she was "on" a bird. Harrison fired the pistol in the air to break her trance.

He sicced thousands of mosquitoes on me. I let them bite. Did not flinch.

He showed me the crushed high grass where a black bear had recently passed. In his red Toyota Land Cruiser, he played eerie tapes of wolves howling. He was a gamer, all right.

We went to the Dunes saloon for the traditional post-fight nightcap amid his entourage of local admirers.

I ended up lying on my stomach on the breakwall in Grand Marais Bay, looking down at the water, waiting for the sun to come up, computing the final point tally for the event.

Me 136, him 134.

Really, a big come-from-behind win for the underdog kid from Detroit. Thank you, Bill Yeats.

It helped, of course, to be the one keeping score.

Schizophrenic's Song

Four months ago, the big man got trapped again in a waking nightmare.

He felt a sudden urge to drive, so he climbed into his car in Milwaukee and a moment later (so it seemed to him) was in a town five hours away. He tried to settle into a motel room for the night, but the room was filled with voices. He needed to escape.

The next thing he knew, it was 4 in the morning and he was walking down a dark, unfamiliar road. Each time a car passed, jabbering people rose from the cracks in the pavement. He came upon the form of a large man lying face down on the side of the roadway: himself.

"But it wasn't scary," Lionel Aldridge insisted. "It's not scary to me anymore. I've been making a real effort to recover from this illness and it's not to my advantage to be frightened by the hallucinations."

Not to his advantage.

Sports fans may remember Lionel Aldridge. He was a starting defensive end for the Green Bay Packers in the halcyon years of coach Vince Lombardi, during which the team won Super Bowls I and II. But "former football player" is not how he characterizes himself these days.

"My diagnosis is paranoid-schizophrenic," he said by way of introducing himself to a roomful of mental health workers at Catherine McAuley Health Center near Ann Arbor. "You can ask me any questions you've always wanted to ask your own clients but feared might hurt them. I'm not having any symptoms right now. At the moment I'm completely symptom-free."

One's own serious mental illness is perhaps the hardest affliction to look in the eye. Admitting you're crazy, after all, fully separates you from virtually all other human beings; it requires a special bigness.

Physically, Lionel Aldridge fills the bill. He is 6 feet 4 and, at age 48, many pounds above his playing weight of 245 pounds. He is kind-spoken and articulate, his hands huge and well groomed. When he speaks of his schizophrenia, he smiles a great deal, yet seems sometimes not far from tears.

Over 12 years beginning in 1974, Aldridge lost a marriage and an established career in sports broadcasting to terrifying voices and shadowy human forms in places reason told him were unoccupied. Fear, paranoia, the growing inability to control his actions — these were a pack of dogs that hounded him out of rational society and into the streets.

In 1983, Jet magazine depicted him living in the Milwaukee Rescue Mission. Ashamed, he dropped from sight for more than two years, wandering from city to city in the company of his agonies.

It was not until 1986 that Aldridge finally sought treatment. Since then, psychotropic drugs have largely erased the hallucinations (the experience four months ago was his first "episode" in three years).

The most astonishing thing about his turnaround, however, is the way he has willed it.

Lately, Aldridge has been making a living giving motivational speeches. He does best, he says, talking to fellow schizophrenics and their families. He is much less comfortable appearing before mental health professionals and must battle the schizophrenic's urge to withdraw.

Before his talk at McAuley Health Center cafeteria, he stood alone on an outdoor patio nervously smoking a Camel. Inside, it was cool, but a light film of perspiration glistened on his face as he spoke, and he had to remove his jacket. Several times, he made a point of informing his audience of how he was reacting to them.

"I'm still scared of you guys," he said to McAuley staffers, most of whom were women half his size. "I am, you know. I think you're diagnosing me. ... (then, with complete sincerity) Do you feel I need that? ... I don't feel I'm doing real good with you right now, and I don't know why. The point I'm at right now, I kind of know when I'm having a problem. I'm constantly testing myself to see if I'm all right — whether what I'm doing is what a normal person would do."

Just as he forces himself to cook meals and do dishes and clean his home, he tends to the housework of his mind, which the disease ceaselessly litters with irrational thoughts.

"I know, for example, that anger is not good for me, so I go through a process where I get rid of it," he said. "One of the things I work on is forgiving people. You know, I forgive people for the sins they commit *in my mind*. In other words, I forgive them for what I think they are thinking. Otherwise, I could be tied up for several days on just what I think you were thinking of me.

"I even have fun with that. I laugh at some of the silly things I think people might be thinking of me. I have to do it to keep me light and to keep me positive and to keep me from having a problem."

Even familiar people and places, he said, must regularly be purged of the dangers his mind would ascribe to them. He cited the case of a restaurant near his home where he frequently goes for coffee. From time to time he finds himself standing outside the windows of the place and starting to think that "nobody inside that restaurant wants me in there.

"But if I turn around at that point and go back home, I'm allowing the illness to limit my life. Instead of that, I just start to imagine that I like me. That I love me. And I take me on into that restaurant. Maybe not real steady. But I sit me down and I continue to imagine that I like myself. Pretty soon, the waitress is treating me like *she* likes me. And then somebody's talking to me about football, and it's real obvious to me that none of those people in that restaurant knew that they didn't want me in there."

The roots of this resolve, he said, lie in his pro football career, when the storied Lombardi trained him to banish any thoughts that weren't conducive to winning the next Sunday's game.

Aldridge's present struggle is far more valorous. The opposition, unlike John Unitas or Don Meredith, cannot be laid hold of and taken down before the verifying eyes of thousands of people.

Plus, every day is Game Day, and the season lasts the rest of his life.

The Skinny on Souter

Possessed again by the ghost of Robert Leslie Bellem (1902-1968), creator of legendary hard-boiled pulp-mag detective Dan Turner ...

The slit-eyed dick at the gate lamped my papers for a long time. I set fire to a gasper and tried not to blow too much smoke in his mug.

"Turner, eh?" he said. "To see who?"

I straightened the brim of my hat. "You probably heard of him. The Large Potato. The Head Cheese." I pointed to the invitation embossed with "The White House, Washington."

He escorted me around back of the place and into the big, egg-shaped office.

The Main Noise sat behind a desk, looking at me like I should take my hat off. Fat chance of that. I crushed the coffin nail out on the carpet and took a seat. "What's the skinny?" I asked.

"The Souter thing," he said. "My Supreme Court nominee. Gotta check for hidden dirt. The background thing."

"Yeah, but why a low-rent shamus like me? This place is crawling with gumfoots who wear real tin. Besides, newshounds from every blat in the country're on the case."

He took a heavy wad of geetus from a drawer and pushed it toward me.

I looked at the pile of simoleons, then at him. "Taxpayers'?"

He closed his eyes and nodded.

Soon I was on a train to New Hampshire to pay the Souter lug a surprise visit.

I read his file on the way: Harvard. Oxford. Churchgoing. Ascetic. Never married. Lived alone on a farm, reading Jane Austen.

It didn't add up. That wasn't like any gavel-pounder I knew.

I got off at a jerkwater town in the hills and set out on foot. There was a fork in the road. I went right and entered some thick woods. I heard a rustle nearby, and what should come ankling my way but a taffy-haired morsel in a short skirt and spiked heels. She was packing a Tommy gun as big as a side of beef, and seemed to be patrolling.

When she saw me, she raised the gat, but I swatted it away. We wrestled to the ground and I pinned her.

"All right," I said. "Where is he?"

Her bosom heaved beneath her low-cut blouse like fresh loaves of bread. Her blue glims puddled with brine. "You'll never get it out of me!" she cried.

Just then somebody dealt me a wallop to the brain case. It sent me tumbling end over appetite into a bottomless black pool that gulped me like an oyster.

As I was coming to, I heard voices. I pinned the groggy swivel on a skinny joe with a chin like a mouse's. It was Souter, all right. And he wasn't alone.

I'd lamped many a wren in my time, but none as gorgeous as the half-dozen Amazons who were with Souter. He had one on each arm. Two others sat at his feet, their gams tucked appetizingly beneath them. Two more stood over me with rodericks aimed at my attic.

"So, Mr. Turner," the little bozo said. "Did you really think a man of my achievements would be content sitting around a farmhouse alone?"

They all laughed. I tried to raise my head, but a stiletto-heeled foot smushed my kisser to the ground. "Bu', wha' m'I shuppozhed tell zhe White Houzhe?" I said.

He chuckled. "Why, nothing, Mr. Turner. We'll just let this be our little secret, shall we? I'll soon be in a position where I can be very useful to you. I don't think, for example, you'd ever again have to worry about having your license pulled."

He had a point.

"Send Mr. Turner on his way," he told the two tantalizing gunsels. "I know a reasonable man when I see one."

He and the other quails strolled off. I heard one say drippingly, "My turn tonight, Your Honor."

"And mine," said another.

"A turn for everyone," he said, laughing. "Equal protection under the law, my dears."

I got up, straightened my hat and torched another gasper.

I thought, strict constructionist my foot.

Resurrection

For a couple of months now, for reasons I don't entirely understand, I've been thinking a lot about Tommy Mastroianni.

He was my very good friend during the very best phase of boyhood, the last years before the revolution and chaos of the teens.

Tommy and his large, close-knit family moved into our sooty neighborhood in Steubenville, Ohio, when I was about 10. He was a stocky boy, calm and likable and devoid of the bellicosity that marked most of the other boys growing up within walking distance of the brooding Wheeling Steel plant.

I'd never felt comfortable among them. It was no wonder I liked "Maz" so much so fast.

Those summers, all that mattered was baseball. We played in the yard of Washington School every day it didn't rain. We followed with passion every twist and turn of the Pittsburgh Pirates' fate. Major league night games were just becoming common on television. Tommy and I would lie on our bellies on the speckled linoleum floor of his darkened TV room, transfixed by the gray-and-white images of Bill Virdon and Roberto Clemente, surrounded by the soft, black, open-windowed, cricket-chirping night.

Tommy could murder a baseball. He had the perfect hitter's body, heavy-legged, low to the ground, powerful. Me, I couldn't hit to save my soul. My incompetence at the plate was the shame of my Little League career.

One game, however, I managed three solid hits with a brand-new black Louisville Slugger. My coach, hoping against hope, let me take the bat home to practice with. Tommy was very impressed by it and I let him borrow it for one of his Little League games.

That night, he showed up on our porch, still in uniform, his face funereal. One shard of the bat was in his right hand, the other in his left. I tried to be angry with him, but couldn't sustain it. He was too easy to forgive.

Our friendship ebbed after my family moved to a newer part of town late in my eighth-grade school year. Tommy and I went to different high schools and rarely bumped into each other.

But I kept hearing about him over the years. I heard he'd married soon after graduating. I heard he'd gone to work. I heard he'd been drafted and shipped overseas and that his wife was pregnant.

Then, a few months before I was to graduate from college, I heard he'd been killed in Vietnam.

One afternoon last week, 22 years late, I began calling around my hometown to learn details of Tommy's brief adult life, and to say to his family that I have been thinking about him.

"Yes, we think of him a lot, too," said Tommy's mother, Katie, whose voice I'd not heard in three decades. "He died March 19, 1967. It happened in Quang Tri. He was wounded one time before that, so he got two Purple Hearts. I have all the papers and letters they sent me and we've got them all put away. All I know is, he used to go into the helicopters, then they'd drop them off. They'd jump out, and that's how he got hurt the first time. He hurt his ankle."

Tommy's widow's name was Sharon, Katie Mastroianni told me. She'd been only 16 when he died; he'd been 20. Three years after Tommy's death, she'd wed Tommy's older brother, Nick, and they were married still.

With Katie's help, I got in touch with Sharon and asked her about the moment when she learned of Tommy's death.

"I was at my mother-in-law's house on Fifth Street near Holy Name Cathedral," she said. "It was in the evening and some of my girlfriends from school were there. I hadn't seen them for a long time and, for some reason, they stopped to see me. We were sitting around the dining room table, and there was a knock on the door. I went to answer it and I saw my mom and my dad and my sister..."

Here she had to stop, swallow and recompose herself.

"... I thought they had come just to see me, you know? But then I saw the Marine sergeant standing behind them.

"He was the first boy from around here to be killed, and that brought it home. You heard things every day about people dying over there, but when this happened, well, the war was here now."

A month after Tommy went to Vietnam, Sharon gave birth to their child. It was a boy, and they named him Thomas Michael. His father never saw him. "Tommy Michael," as his immediate family calls him, is 22, Sharon said, 5 feet 8 and about 175 pounds.

"He resembles his father exactly and is real easygoing; he can get anybody to do anything," she said. He lives at home with his mother and Nick while finishing junior college.

Tommy Mastroianni came on the line.

"Everyone tells me I look just like him," he said affably. "But I never knew my real father. This (Nick) is the one I know. He's been my father to me, and we have a great relationship."

I thought I could hear a little of Tommy in his son's voice, but I may have been listening too hard for the similarity.

He told me he'd been a starting defensive back for the football team of Wintersville High School, from which he'd graduated in 1985. As for baseball, he'd never played beyond Babe Ruth League — "a better fielder than hitter," he explained.

I asked if he sometimes looks at old photographs and wonders about his biological father.

"Oh, yeah. A lot of times," he said. "I wonder what kind of relationship we'd have had, what he'd be like to talk to, how strict he would be with me. Would he give me a lot of leeway? Spoil me rotten?"

It felt weird, he said, to think he was already older than his father ever got.

"I'm only a month away from my associate degree," he said. "I'm almost done. I'm hoping to go two more years to get my bachelor's in law enforcement up at Ohio State, and then maybe get into the FBI or another government job. That's what I'm hoping."

The only way the living deal well with the dead is through a sense of future.

That is why Memorial Day exists. We'd be overwhelmed by the thought of 540,000 countrymen who have died in combat since 1775 if we couldn't think they have continuing relevance to our national life, our independence, our psychological unity and so on.

I think something like this explains why Tommy Mastroianni was so troubling my mind. I had let him simply cease. His memory had not had, for me, a specific connection to the future.

Now it has.

Peace, Tommy.

AT HOME

CHAPTER SEVEN

In Perfect Alignment

Nothing a person can do around the house reflects human existence as precisely as wallpapering.

Neither linoleum-tile laying nor drain unclogging nor electrical rewiring are as rich in symbolism (although drain unclogging comes close).

Only those whose passion for experiencing life keeps them from giving hundreds of dollars to strangers to redecorate their houses are privy to wallpapering's secret truths.

Wallpapering can seem at first nothing more than a tedium whose purpose is to prettify the vertical surfaces of a room. Your average beginner, on realizing the flowers aren't lining up right, is likely not only to wish he or she had paid the extra hundreds of dollars, but to overlook the hidden messages, too.

Like life, wallpapering is all about the tricky matching of things. It is all about anticipating so as not to come up short or look foolish; about trimming excess and tucking mistakes into corners and other places where they're least noticeable.

Most importantly, it is about rectitude. Straightness is the heart and soul of wallpapering.

You start with a true vertical line, made with a plumb or level, on a clean stretch of wall. Sort of like being born.

You stick the first strip of paper so that its edge is along this line. This assures that subsequent strips, like the easy days of childhood, go up straight.

Eventually, however, you come to a corner, and once you turn it, the world is a different place.

Corners are disillusioning. Despite their appearance, they are never perfectly square. A strip of paper begun straight on the first wall ends up crooked on the next wall after it traverses a corner.

The only way to deal with this is to draw another true vertical line on the second wall, lay a strip of paper along it and cut this piece where it overlaps the crooked one. This always messes up the pattern near the corner, but it is better than just continuing on, getting crookeder and crookeder. You cut so as to make the imperfection as obscure as possible, but you cannot make it invisible; it is a reality scar.

Corners are kind of like the complicating passages of life. First, adolescence; then, parenthood, middle age, divorce, empty nest, retirement, whatever. Each is an unsettling transformation, a permanent interruption of the nice, straight lines of the previous phase. Each requires a re-establishment of your plumb line if you're to make it down the next stretch of wall with rectitude.

Of course, the analogy between wallpapering and life eventually breaks down on this point: Life has a Last Corner that you can't see around, and no length of paper can straddle.

Which raises the whole question of what sort of Final Plumb Line, or ultimate setting of things straight, gets drawn on the other side of it.

That, however, is a religious consideration, and religion is much more like roofing than it is like wallpapering.

This Bulb's a Turn-on

Those scientists who gathered in Washington recently to report on the beneficial effects of garlic got most of it right.

Researchers at the First World Congress on the Health Significance of Garlic described animal tests that indicate garlic keeps down cholesterol and triglycerides, prevents blood clots, helps dissolve arterial blockages, keeps normal cells from turning cancerous and protects cells from damage by all sorts of industrial pollutants.

Being men and women of mere science, however, they didn't even get into the emotional and erotic aspects of garlic.

Fortunately, I am eminently qualified, both by ethnic upbringing and loyally maintained familiarity with the substance, to fill this informational gap. That's all right. You don't have to thank me.

My lifelong commitment to garlic began when I was a small child. My family was in the habit of dropping by my grandmother's house after church on Sunday mornings. Part of the ritual was tasting the meatballs my grandmother cooked in the great cauldron of spaghetti sauce that chuckled on her stove each Sabbath. She'd ladle a meatball onto a plate, smear it with some of the sauce and lay a thick slice of homemade bread next to it. This was sometimes accompanied by a small glass of my grandfather's homemade wine.

Well, when you split that loosely packed morsel with your fork, hot, perfumed ghosts of garlic rose and enveloped your face.

I was imprinted with the smell. To this day, there is no food aroma that so transports me as that of a scattering of finely chopped garlic frizzling in a shallow lake of hot olive oil at the bottom of a cast-iron skillet. It fills a house with the promise of feasting, whetting the appetite for all that will be sauteed with it or combined with it to form sauces and braising liquids for meats.

And that's not all it whets the appetite for.

I don't know how the scientists could have overlooked this, but garlic is pretty clearly a love potion, a subtle but effective aphrodisiac. Personal experience has convinced me of this.

A woman with the smell of garlic on her hands — yee-ow — I am hers. I am instantly persuaded of her earth-grounded, man-tending powers. It must go back to my grandmother somehow. Further, I find that when I cook and get the aroma on my own fingers — well, how can I put this discreetly — my thoughts begin to wander pret-ty darned widely among the opposite gender.

You'll see.

Here is a recipe I'd like you to try. It's for a simple garlic, tomato and fresh basil sauce from Marcella Hazan, the doyenne of Italian cooking. It is meant to be tossed with about a pound of cooked thin pasta called spaghettini. No cheese is to be used.

Combine in a saucepan 5 cloves of finely chopped garlic, 1½ cups of coarsely chopped fresh basil leaves, 2 cups of canned Italian plum tomatoes (drained, seeded and coarsely chopped), ⅓ cup of olive oil, half a dozen twists of freshly ground pepper and 1 teaspoon of salt. Cook uncovered over medium-high heat for 15 minutes.

That's it.

Oops, I almost forgot: Stir occasionally with a wooden spoon. It should come in handy also for fending off amorous persons in the neighborhood.

A Real Saab Story

I recently learned on the very same day that:

a.) One of every nine Iowans gives his or her car a name; and

b.) Ford Motor Co. has been negotiating to buy into Saab-Scania, the Swedish automaker.

What a coincidence. I have owned eight cars in my life, and only one affected me so personally that I bestowed a name on it. It was a used 1977 Saab 99 GLE I dubbed "The Swedish Meatball."

Like all Saabs, it was oddly fishlike in shape, sturdy in an old-fashioned way, relentlessly sensible. A car engineered by your mother so you wouldn't get hurt.

When I bought it in 1985, the Meatball was a sight to behold. One of a run of Saabs that had been assembled in Belgium and undergone a defective metal pre-paint process, it had huge, painful looking ulcers on its fenders, doors and roof. The rest of its skin was a brownish maroon so dull it did not reflect light. I bought it for $1,000 from a friend whose high-toned Birmingham neighbors had sicced the police on him for keeping it parked in front of his home.

The previous owner warned me of electrical problems. It being Swedish, I figured it occasionally got depressed, like in Ingmar Bergman movies. But I lucked into a Syrian mechanic on Woodward Avenue who diagnosed an incorrect ignition coil, and for $9 had the car running like an athlete.

I thus had to cope with a profound duality.

On the one hand, the car's interior was immaculate and comfortable. It had a complete emergency backup brake system. Its handling was nimble and precise. Even at high speeds it sat on the road with the weighty authority of an old Lincoln. No matter how frigid the weather, it started eagerly; electric coils instantly warmed the driver's seat (thanks, Mom).

On the other hand, the Meatball blighted any landscape it traversed. People stopped and turned to watch it go by. My children insisted on being let off a block from wherever I was taking them so they wouldn't be seen in it by their friends.

Owning the Meatball was like loving a good-hearted but grotesquely deformed person. I came to scorn the astonishment of people who looked at us. The Meatball became a sort of cause with me.

The car had 56,000 miles on the odometer when I bought it, and I drove it another 33,000. Although its cancer worsened, its mechanical heart beat on heroically.

In the spring of 1988, having tired of all the psychological stress, I sold the Meatball to a friend for $450. I can't honestly say I miss the sight of it in my driveway, but somehow I miss its presence in my life.

Now I drive a stripped-down 1988 economy car that is light of weight and smooth of skin, and will probably dice me into neat cubes if it ever collides with anything. I've tried to think up a name for it, but nothing comes to mind.

The present owner of the Meatball, meanwhile, reports he has driven it another 15,000 miles. Now, alas, it is "in sick bay" with fuel-injection problems. If he can't get them fixed economically, he says, he's going to junk it.

If it were mine, I'd do things differently. I'd deck it out in flags and tow it past the defunct garage of the disappeared Syrian mechanic. I'd parade it through the neighborhood where it once got ticketed for being ugly. Then I'd abandon it in downtown Birmingham.

The Weigh of All Flesh

Having just eaten our way unawares through most of National Eating Disorders Awareness Week, perhaps we ought to make some sort of appropriate gesture before it's too late.

I suggest this: Throwing away our bathroom scales.

I recently parted with my own and can testify to the liberating effect of not knowing one's weight.

Our preoccupation with weight has long since gone too far. Not, of course, for those whose extreme avoirdupois is a direct threat to their health, but certainly for the great majority of us, the weight-concerned.

How bad things have gotten is suggested by a recent study of more than 900 freshmen women at the University of Michigan. It found that more than 80 percent of them were dieters, and almost 40 percent fell into the categories of intense dieters, dieters-at-risk (who empty their stomachs by vomiting or using laxatives, or take appetite suppressants or diuretics) and binge-and-purge bulimics.

What a weightist society can wring in the psyches of young women, who are already predisposed by sexist propaganda not to like the way they look, is infuriating. It causes those of us with teenage daughters to live in fear.

My own tale of the scale began when I was 27. Seven years of eating as though I were still a teenager — which is to say, like a tree chipping machine — had me blossoming all around the middle. So I bought an inexpensive scale at a drugstore, put myself on a homemade diet, started exercising again and eventually dropped 25 pounds.

During this time I acquired the habit of weighing in each morning as soon as I awoke. The initial exhilaration of those early days of watching the numbers go down turned out to have a very high price: sixteen years of petty tyranny, of fretful self-accusation whenever the fine red needle ratcheted a little more eastward than usual along the little calibrated lines. It came to feel as though I was measuring my very character and worth, instead of my base meat.

A few months ago, no doubt weary from the stress of its long tenure exercising all this power over my life, my scale died.

At first, it seemed strange not knowing how much of me there was from one day to the next. I told myself I'd buy a new scale, this time a real good one with a digital readout. But that thought proved no match for the expanding sense of relief I'd begun to feel almost from the moment I put the old thing out with the trash.

By now my attitude has completely changed. I say the hell with scales and the whole narcissistic preoccupation they represent. I look at the scratched place on the bathroom tile where the scale used to be and wonder how I ever let such an oppressor into my home.

There are other ways to sense our physical waxing and waning. The waistbands of our clothes tell us accurately enough when we should lay off the beer and pretzels. People we know and love keep us sufficiently apprised of the state of our appearance.

We ought to save rigorous, daily self-calibration for what really matters — the mass of our goodwill, the volume of our benevolence, the breadth of our open-mindedness.

Give me an instrument that measures these, and I'll gladly step onto it each morning.

Shellfish Gestures

Ordinarily, I refrain from committing murder, but, see, we have this tradition.

In my household, when it's your birthday or other special day, you get to pick what you want for dinner and the others have to make it for you.

Last Sunday, Mother's Day, my spouse ordered a dish she'd seen in a fancy cookbook and long had been eager to try. I found, to my chagrin, it called for, among other things, one live lobster.

Now, I've eaten lobster in restaurants, but I'd never cooked a live one before. My spouse said it would be fine with her if we used canned or frozen lobster meat, but when it comes to cookbooks, I am a fundamentalist. I cleave to Holy Writ and steer clear of the pitfalls of interpretationism. It is one of my most profound inflexibilities. Live means live.

So I went to the supermarket and picked a candidate from among the plump black-and-gold crustaceans fidgeting in the seafood cooler. "Euwwwww. Imagine eating that thing," said a woman standing near me as the clerk slid the lobster into a thick plastic bag.

"Ohhh, hel-lo, Mr. Lobster. Hel-lo-oo. Awwww," cooed the young woman at the checkout counter, holding the bagged creature up close to her face. "Hey, Louie! Louie the Lobster," called the bag boy. Neither would look at me.

I was starting to feel bad about this. Sort of like a few Easters ago when, the cruel irony having been completely lost on me until it was too late, I'd cooked braised rabbit for dinner.

As I drove away, the lobster crinkled accusingly in the grocery bag on the seat next to me.

"I said you could use canned lobster," my spouse said self-absolvingly when I got home. "I hope this is not a mother lobster."

"He looks so sad," my older daughter added helpfully.

I placed the twitching thing on a package of sliced salami in the refrigerator and put a large pot of water on the stove. The anxiety in the kitchen rose with the water temperature. No watched pot ever took longer to boil. To distract myself, I read up on proper procedure: "... immerse the lobster in the water head first to minimize splashing. ..." Great. The poor thing was going to thrash and writhe. We were going to have a death scene of operatic proportions. Plus, the lobster was going to make a piteous shriek, or at least that's what I heard they did.

sssssSSSSS said the steam escaping from beneath the lid of the pot.

With elaborate care, which is to say, procrastination, I squeezed half a lemon over the pot, added a few sprigs of parsley and some cayenne pepper.

This was it.

I snipped the bag open and gingerly picked the lobster up at the waist; one of his antennae flopped back, trustingly, I loathed to think, against my wrist. I carried it to the stove. We humans gathered grimly for the execution.

I tensed my jaws and pushed the lobster in headfirst.

He didn't splash. He didn't shriek. He went quietly, rolling over on his back and beginning obediently to turn red. One of his little legs straightened and its tip stuck out from beneath the simmering water.

"He's signaling, 'Help! Help!' " said my daughter.

"He's giving you the finger," said my spouse.

I envisioned his ghost going up in a cloud of lobster fume. I was so glad this was over.

Five minutes later, red and cooling on a cutting board, he was a lot easier to look at. A small bright bit of my emotional history.

But at the dinner table, I have to admit, the sweetness of his meat was tinged with a certain ashiness, in my mouth at least.

Being the non-mother parental unit, I did the dishes afterward. Through the window, I watched a fat robin pull an earthworm from the ground at the edge of the patio, snip it into sections and devour it. Alive.

At least I'd spared the lobster that indignity, I told myself.

Still, come Father's Day, I'm going with salmon fillets, nice, safe and thoroughly deceased at someone else's hand.

That Sinking Feeling

In our very homes, we exist alongside a parallel universe, a separate dimension of reversed logic, weirdly named oddments and incomprehensible laws.

It is called plumbing.

Sometimes this universe requires human intervention. It is most unwise to make any such trespass lightly.

A plumbing repair task, no matter how small, carries the seed of infinite expansion. Fertilized with the right combination of inadequate tools and undiscerning workperson, it can grow into a monster capable of devouring a weekend's worth of good mood.

At stake is a household's sense of civilization. Without showers, without flushable toilets, barbarism is at the door. Especially if teenagers live in the house.

Last weekend I decided to take on a bathroom sink faucet that dripped at penetrating volume through the night. As an experienced homeowner, I felt justified in attempting so small and familiar a task as replacing the washers in a leaky tap. Still, I moved with caution. I was going to do this right the first time, so as to miss only a little of the Michigan-Illinois game on TV.

At my place, you have to turn off the water for the entire house to work on any faucet. I took advantage of the fact that my spouse was out and the teenage component of the household still was fast asleep, it being but 1 in the afternoon.

I turned off the water in the basement, loped up two flights of stairs, took apart the two faucets and drove the old washers to the hardware store to make sure I got proper replacements. I was back in a flash, installed the new washers, put the faucets back together, buffed the chrome a little and danced downstairs to turn the water back on.

The faucet leaked worse than before.

I plodded to the basement and turned off the water, chagrined. Upstairs, I took everything apart again. I pounded downstairs and out to the car, taking the innards of the hot water faucet with me to the hardware man.

"Bad diverter seat," he said, in the language of the parallel universe. He replaced the small part. I drove home and reassembled everything again.

Still, the leak.

I telephoned the hardware man, explaining as evenly as I could manage that it "... did ... not ... work."

I would have to buy a whole new faucet valve. I checked on the teenage component. Still drowned in adolescent repose. Stairs. Water off. Car. Hardware store. Home. Stairs. Reassemble. Stairs. Water on. Stairs.

Leak.

Stairswateroffeverythingapartagain. Groggy teenager whining about shower. Has a date later. Going to have to go dirty? Gaw-awd.

I sat on the ceramic tile floor, a valve in each hand, and meditated on the objects, silently imploring them to give up their secrets. This is my last-resort approach to plumbing.

Finally, I noticed the older valve was missing a small metal cap over the diverter. I found what looked like the cap in the wastebasket, reassembled the hardware and trudged, without much hope, downstairs. I turned on the water.

The leak was history.

So, unfortunately, was the football game.

I did get a final score, however.

Parallel U 1, Homeowner 0.

Sole of a Gentleman

I am generally reluctant to have my shoes shined. I've always felt there is something anti-democratic about a fellow American cleaning and polishing my footwear while I'm still in it. I think the shiner, no matter how outwardly friendly, resents the heck out of it and, as he rubs the polish into the leather, is fantasizing about slitting my throat from ear to ear.

Urgent necessity has forced me into the shoe-shine chair a few times, however. By far the best shine I ever got was in the airport of booming Charlotte, N.C. It cost only $3, and given the quality of the work (and the magnitude of my guilt) I tipped like a rock star.

Charlotte may call itself "The Corporate Center of the Future South" or "The City Run by White Protestant Males," or whatever its Chamber of Commerce likes it to go by, but for me it will always be "The City of Glistening Loafers."

I usually feel compelled to attend to the care of my shoes myself, working them over once or twice a year whether they need it or not. On a bottom shelf of my closet is a large sturdy box filled with brushes, cans, small glass jars and a dozen rags stiffly clotted with dried polish the color of blood, of ink, of, uh, certain organic wastes. Its sharp, waxy smell is to me as male a scent as pipe tobacco.

When I was a small boy, all shoe shining in the household was tended to by my father. I have vivid memories of my brother and me standing on kitchen chairs while the old man vigorously snapped a cloth over the toes of our dress shoes and lectured on the fine art of paste-waxing.

The subtext we picked up was that classily civilized man gives in neither to the ubiquitous dusts of the earth nor to quick-fix liquid polishes that make shoes look like old cars that have been repainted with a brush.

I think this was the case in most families then. A friend who comes from a large family says he and his brothers were required to polish their shoes each Saturday night and submit them to their father for inspection.

Why this should be so male a chore, I'm not quite sure. It probably has something to do with three generations of drill sergeants threatening that they'd better be able to shave in the reflection of those boots, soldier. All I know is, whenever I'm discovered in the act, females of the household begin lining up footwear within my reach, as though the obligation to shine were a natural and inescapable part of having Y-chromosomes. No wonder I think twice a year is plenty often enough.

Apparently, I am part of an alarming downward trend in male self-respect. In what I am sure was an excruciatingly scientific survey of business personnel specialists (it was sponsored by Kiwi Brands), 43 percent of respondents said less than half of the male management-position applicants they see have newly shined shoes. Dull shoes were the single most common defect in appearance, ahead of even bad posture and failure to make eye contact.

"If they didn't take time to check out their shoes, they would not be a candidate for an executive-level position," said one personnel type with dark finality.

Wow. A further diminution of the executive pool, as if American business didn't already have enough to worry about.

No wonder so many companies are moving their headquarters to Charlotte.

Freedom Has a Ring to It

My late father-in-law, a tough old steel-mill foreman with a voice like an underground nuclear explosion, hated the telephone. Generally, he refused to answer it at home. The most common exception was when it rang during dinner, at which times he'd snatch up the receiver, roar, "We're eating," then hang up without further nicety.

He was of an earlier generation, and he resented the gratuitous disruption that noisy emissary of the outside world could inflict on the peace and tranquillity of his household. For all the convenience it offered, it was still a dagger pointed at the heart of his privacy.

Like everyone else in the family, I used to look on his phone-hating with great amusement.

That is, until I started refusing to answer telephones myself.

I don't recall exactly when this first happened, but it was some time during the last two years. I was in the recliner listening to music. No one else was home. I was very comfortable. When the phone went off and my muscles twitched in conditioned response to raise me up, a wondrous insight flashed through my mind:

This is my chair. This is my music. This is my reverie. Why in the world should I leap up from them just because a small machine nagged from the kitchen wall? If the call were important, the caller surely would try again before long; maybe by then it would be convenient, maybe it would please me, to answer.

The phone rang and rang, and then it stopped. I've felt a little more in command of my existence ever since.

As usual, I am moving in the opposite direction from a social trend. Americans are spending more time on the horn now than ever before (3.017 trillion minutes in 1980, 3.754 trillion in 1987, according to the Federal Communications Commission).

More than two million people currently subscribe to cellular service, so they can have phones in their cars and on their laps at their kids' soccer games. I imagine I might like being able to contact anyone I wish at any time, but I couldn't abide the concurrent increase in my own net reachability.

Personally, I sort of like being unreachable from time to time, such as when I'm daydreaming or zipping along in my car listening to classic rock and consulting with myself on how the old life is coming along.

We are almost completely inured to the ringing telephone. We don't think of it as beckoning, but of commanding immediate response. We allow it to take instant priority over everything else. We may be having the most important domestic confrontation of our lives, yet we will abruptly suspend it to give some idiot selling magazines a shot at our ears.

It takes nerves of steel to ignore a ringing telephone, but it is an exercise in mental discipline I highly recommend. Turning off the phone or diverting calls to an answering machine is not as valuable. The benefit of letting a phone ring is in knowing someone's trying to invade your life and choosing not to permit it. It does wonders for your self-esteem.

Try it sometime when you're in a contemplative mood. When the little monster jangles, count the rings the way people who meditate count their breaths. Speculate on the identity of the privacy invader you're foiling. Quell the guilt in your stomach, and stay put.

Unless, of course, I happen to be the one who's calling.

POSTCARD

My Michigan

Having just driven 1,700 miles around this state's two peninsulas, I am more mindful than usual of how much I've come to love Michigan.

And I'm a graduate of Ohio State.

Writing this, I am sitting on the deck of some friends' cottage in Charlevoix County overlooking a deep, clear, spring-fed lake. The morning is overcast and calm and exceptionally quiet. The lake looks like forest-green gelatin; in the distance, two kids in a yellow canoe crease the surface. The water is sweet-tasting and clean enough to drink.

Yeah, it's the water, all right, that stole my affections. You do not get water like this in my native Ohio. Not unless you buy it in bottles.

The poisons of the convenience society long since have sullied the Great Lakes, with only Superior still holding its own. Nonetheless, I can't stare at Lake Michigan on Point Betsie, or at the straits near St. Ignace, or at Superior from the Pictured Rocks without trying to imagine the thoughts of the first saltwater-faring Europeans as they first laid eyes on these breathless expanses of water. Mon dieu. And every drop drinkable. Every drop akin to 80 percent of our physical natures.

Driving up the western edge of the Keweenaw Peninsula last week for the first time, I stopped to gaze at the gigantic horseshoe of Great Sand Bay. Superior was incomparably blue and perking with whitecaps. The sun was bright. The entire bowl of bay was lined with light, velvety sand. Yet there was no one on the spectacular beach below.

I thought the day might come when crowded, droughty southern California is a char, and its moneyed people and hyperkinetic developers will seek the emptiness and verdancy of places like this.

Probably a groundless fear. The snows will keep them away. In early August, it's easy to forget the mountains of cold white that will begin accumulating here in a matter of 12 or 13 weeks, to abide for half a year. No perennial adolescent summer here.

Not only the water, however, has kept me smitten with Michigan. Its various places and peoples seem to me more intriguingly different from one another than is the case in, say, Ohio. I mean, the thought of the denizens of a Detroit jazz club and those of a Finnlander bar in Calumet paying overly high taxes to the same state government is a little boggling.

Even Michigan's history is part of the love mix. It is big, harsh and epoch-making, and I feel its effects in the present wherever I go in the state, much more keenly than I ever feel Ohio's when I'm traveling there.

I cannot drive the bridge over Henry Ford's Rouge plant and not feel at a loss as to how human beings could have conceived and built it.

I cannot visit Hartwick Pines without feeling a powerful ache for the loss of the mammoth old pine forests obliterated two generations before I was even born.

And, despite all the tourist-targeted boosterism of "Copper Country," I couldn't traipse the Keweenaw last week without being a little astounded by the currency that paid for the copper boom of late last century.

In little Evergreen Cemetery outside Eagle River, four of the first six gravestones I read said this:

"In memory of Tom Harper, Who Was Killed by the Falling of a Rock in the Phoenix Mine, June 21, 1876, Age 19 Years...."

"Henry Hart, Killed at Copper Falls Mine July 15, A.D. 1872, Age 21 Years...."

"James, Beloved Son of Edward Fezzey, Killed at Copper Falls Mine July 15, A.D. 1872, Age 19 Years and 8 Months...."

"James Trebilcock, Son of Marmaduke and Mary Trebilcock, Died at Cliff (Mine), January 24, 1865, Age 10 Years, 2 Months...."

Of such mortar was the foundation of Michigan's economy constructed.

Almost as much as the water, I also relish Michigan's psychic division between downstate and up, even though it makes for some pretty ugly politics in Lansing.

Many natives, I know, yearn for the one region or the other. Burned-out Detroit cops count the days till they can retire to the northern woods. Meanwhile, to some of the unemployed young of the north, Detroit and environs still look like the City on the Hill (the main downtown streets of both Houghton and Hancock in beautiful Keweenaw have St. Vincent De Paul stores).

Personally I love going back and forth across the line. If there is stress and jeopardy below it, there is refuge above. If there is neediness and boredom above, there is opportunity and excitement below.

Back and forth. Respite and reinvolvement. Yin and yang.

So much to think about here.

But a hummingbird has just visited, making a soft chirp of disappointment at not finding the feeder my friends used to keep on the deck.

Not only that, but a stand of birches nearby continues its glacial progress down the bank to the patient water.

I'd better watch a while.